Praise for  **W9-CBI-650**

*25 Questions You're Afraid to Ask about Love, Sex, and Intimacy*

There's a lot more to "the birds and the bees" than understanding human physiology. Our sexuality is intricately connected with our identity, our desires, our sense of self-worth, and even our spiritual health! In this gutsy book, Dr. Juli Slattery is like a trusted friend, experienced counselor, and spiritual mentor to her readers, empowering us to better understand and fully embrace our God-given sexuality.

**KELLI B. TRUJILLO**
Editor, *Today's Christian Woman*

Most of us have questions about sex we never ask. After all, sex is highly personal and can be quite an embarrassing topic! That's what makes this book such a valuable and needed guide. Dr. Juli Slattery isn't afraid to answer tough questions about sex—and she does so with tact, sensitivity, and wisdom.

**ARLENE PELLICANE**
Author, *31 Days to a Happy Husband* and coauthor, *Growing Up Social*

In a generation that is quickly turning its back from God and His standards of morality, there are many questions and areas of confusion for people in regard to sexuality. Dr. Juli Slattery bravely joins the discussion by answering twenty-five of the most asked questions about sex and intimacy. This book could not have come at a better time, and I hope that people find freedom and healing in their sexuality as they go through each chapter.

**JENNIFER SMITH**
Author, *The Unveiled Wife: Embracing Intimacy with God and Your Husband*

# 25 QUESTIONS you're AFRAID to ASK —about— LOVE, SEX, and INTIMACY

## Dr. Juli Slattery

**MOODY PUBLISHERS**

CHICAGO

All Scripture quotations, unless otherwise indicated, are taken from the Holy Bible, New International Version®, NIV®. Copyright © 1973, 1978, 1984, 2011 by Biblica, Inc.™ Used by permission of Zondervan. All rights reserved worldwide. www.zondervan.com. The "NIV" and "New International Version" are trademarks registered in the United States Patent and Trademark Office by Biblica, Inc.™

Scripture quotations marked NASB are taken from the *New American Standard Bible®*, Copyright © 1960, 1962, 1963, 1968, 1971, 1972, 1973, 1975, 1977, 1995 by The Lockman Foundation. Used by permission. (www.Lockman.org)

Scripture quotations marked ESV are from The Holy Bible, English Standard Version® (ESV®), copyright © 2001 by Crossway, a publishing ministry of Good News Publishers. Used by permission. All rights reserved.

Scripture quotations marked (NLT) are taken from the Holy Bible, New Living Translation, copyright © 1996, 2004, 2007 by Tyndale House Foundation. Used by permission of Tyndale House Publishers, Inc., Carol Stream, Illinois 60188. All rights reserved.

Edited by Elizabeth Cody Newenhuyse
Interior design: Erik M. Peterson
Author photo: Cathy Walters Photography
Cover design and Interior art: Connie Gabbert Design & Illustrations
Cover photo of pen copyright © by imagehub/Shutterstock (163979687).
of journal on table by Connie Gabbert. All rights reserved for both.

Library of Congress Cataloging-in-Publication Data

Slattery, Juli
  25 questions you're afraid to ask about love, sex, and intimacy / Dr. Juli Slattery.
     pages cm
  Includes bibliographical references.
  ISBN 978-0-8024-1342-0
  1. Christian women—Religious life. 2. Sex—Religious aspects—Christianity—Miscellanea. I. Title. II. Title: Twenty-five questions you're afraid to ask about love, sex, and intimacy.
  BV4527.S49 2015
  241'.664082—dc23
                                                    2015020685

We hope you enjoy this book from Moody Publishers. Our goal is to provide high-quality, thought-provoking books and products that connect truth to your real needs and challenges. For more information on other books and products written and produced from a biblical perspective, go to www.moodypublishers.com or write to:

Moody Publishers
820 N. LaSalle Boulevard
Chicago, IL 60610

1 3 5 7 9 10 8 6 4 2

*Printed in the United States of America*

TO MIKE:

Swoo, only because of your love and support
can I write and speak on such sensitive topics.
I am so grateful for the journey of marriage
and intimacy God is taking us through!
I love living life with you and I love you!

# Contents

Introduction       9

**QUESTION 1:**
*What's the big deal about sex?*       13

**QUESTION 2:**
*Who are you to judge my sexual choices?*       21

**QUESTION 3:**
*Can I be single and sexual?*       31

**QUESTION 4:**
*Is it wrong to like sex?*       39

**QUESTION 5:**
*And I waited for this?*       47

**QUESTION 6:**
*Why do guys care so much about sex?*       53

**QUESTION 7:**
*What if I want sex more than my husband does?*       61

**QUESTION 8:**
*How adventurous can we be in bed?*       69

**QUESTION 9:**
*Is _____ okay in the bedroom? (You fill in the blank!)*       77

**QUESTION 10:**
*What do my temptations say about me?*       87

**QUESTION 11:**
*How do I get past my shame?*       93

**QUESTION 12:**
*How do I know he is the one?*       101

**QUESTION 13:**
*How far is too far?*       109

**QUESTION 14:**
*Is living together a good test run for marriage?*     117

**QUESTION 15:**
*What if I'm attracted to someone else?*     125

**QUESTION 16:**
*How can I compete with porn?*     133

**QUESTION 17:**
*What's wrong with mommy porn?*     143

**QUESTION 18:**
*Is masturbation a sin?*     151

**QUESTION 19:**
*Can I be godly and gay?*     159

**QUESTION 20:**
*How do I rebuild trust after a betrayal?*     169

**QUESTION 21:**
*Does forgiveness mean I'll be hurt again?*     177

**QUESTION 22:**
*What if I don't like sex?*     183

**QUESTION 23:**
*How do I make time to make love?*     193

**QUESTION 24:**
*How do we fight without hurting each other?*     201

**QUESTION 25:**
*Why wouldn't God want me to be happy?*     209

Final Thoughts     217
Notes     219
Acknowledgments     223

# Introduction

Do you feel at all strange holding this book in your hands? Are you a bit shy to have someone seeing you reading a book about sex? If so, I can relate. Several times, I've worked on this book while flying to and from speaking events. You know how that curious person sitting by you or behind you who tries to see what you're working on? A little embarrassing.

I never dreamed that I would spend so much time reading, writing, thinking, praying, and speaking about sexuality. I do so because God has given me a passion to redeem His design and proclaim His truth in the most intimate area of women's lives.

This book contains twenty-five questions I often get asked about sex and intimacy. Each year, through the ministry of Authentic Intimacy, we speak to thousands of women and hear hundreds of questions. You will read the most commonly asked in the following pages.

I compiled this book knowing that most women won't read it sequentially but will skip around to the questions that look the most interesting or pressing for them. I also chose not to separate the book into questions for married or single women. Why? Because I believe that we sometimes over-segregate women based on their marital status. Women want to have honest conversations and learn from each other. Single women have questions about marriage, and married women can relate to some of the issues with which single women are struggling.

My goal is to have bold conversations in pursuit of truth. Our sexual questions shouldn't be relegated to dark rooms and lonely nights. They need to be spoken and explored, holding up the Word of God as the standard of truth. This book is not the Bible. My desire is to root everything I teach and write about in God's Word, but I am a human, fallen person. If you doubt something you read in this book, please spend time studying the Scriptures and asking God for His wisdom.

Although this book is not a Bible study, I hope that it encourages healthy dialogue among women in your church, neighborhood, and community. Hopefully, this book will equip you in addressing some of the difficult questions in your life and also help you share truth with others. So, if that person sitting next to you on an airplane or in a doctor's office asks about what you are reading, go ahead and tell them!

While I'm not exactly thrilled when people refer to me as a "Christian Dr. Ruth," one thing keeps me going: seeing God bring redemption and healing to His women. I pray that today you are one of them!

DR. JULI SLATTERY

# WHAT'S *the* BIG DEAL *about* SEX?

# 1

I can remember being a teenager, babysitting at my sister's house. On her nightstand, she had a book about sex. I was intrigued; I was curious. I would never have admitted that to anyone back then, but in the privacy of her house I looked through the book. Asking questions outright about sex was just awkward and embarrassing. It seemed easier to find the answers in a book. Librarians will tell you that books on sexuality are not often checked out, but are secretly paged through. The Internet means you can get information without even having to find a book. The topic of sex makes us curious, interested, filled with shame, and sometimes even disgusted.

One look at the marketing techniques of Madison Avenue will tell you that sex is a powerful force. It is used to sell alcohol, cars, and everything else. Television shows and movies are filled with sexual scenes and innuendos. Approximately 15 percent of searches on the Internet are related to porn. Thirty percent of those looking for porn are women.[1]

Because we rarely admit the power of our sexuality, it works in subversive ways, impacting our choices and often becoming a formidable source of temptation and frustration.

### *What you think about sex matters*

Human sexuality is an essential aspect of who we are as children of God. God purposefully created us as sexual beings and intentionally designed our sexuality to be a powerful force. Because Christians often don't talk or teach about sex, women are confused about what to do with their sexuality. The world's resources like random blogs, erotic novels, and women's magazines seem to have more sexual advice than Christian resources. So women are left with the assumption that God just doesn't have that much to say about sex—other than "don't do it until you're married."

I've met hundreds of Christian women who are struggling with sexual issues. In the silence of the church, they are left to sort through harrowing experiences like childhood sexual abuse, exposure to porn, raging temptation, homosexual thoughts, and betrayal in marriage.

Many women feel like sexuality has hijacked their happiness, and it certainly seems to be a barrier to honoring God. We desperately need God's perspective on sexuality. Fortunately, the Bible has a lot to say on the topic. Some of it might surprise you. We all have thoughts and beliefs about sex that are not based on truth. Maybe the lies you believe about sex came from poor teaching (or deafening silence) in religious settings. Wherever the misinformation came from, it impacts the choices we make. Here is a common example:

Kassandra experienced sexual abuse from a boy in the neighborhood. She didn't tell anyone because she was scared and ashamed to admit it to her Christian parents. As a twelve-year-old girl, she drew many conclusions about herself and about sexuality. Without ever voicing these thoughts, she believed lies like "Sex is dirty. I'm damaged goods. The only way I can ever get a boy's attention is through giving him sex. I will never be pure again." As a teenager, Kassandra moved from boy to boy, and had a secret unplanned pregnancy that ended in abortion. Kassandra is now a forty-year-old wife and mother. Even though she looks like a wonderful Christian woman on the outside, these unspoken messages, violations, and secret sins still dominate her thinking and impact her marriage. She loves the Lord and reads the Bible, but she doesn't quite know how to be free from the shame of her past.

I've met many "Kassandras" over the years. Their faces flash before me even now as I write. They don't know how to be free from the bondage of the past. If you truly want to see the gift of sexuality as it was created to be experienced, you must be willing to expose the lies you've believed as measured by the truth of God's Word.

### *You can't separate your sexuality from your spirituality*

Here is perhaps the most profound truth I have learned from studying what God says about sex: Whether you are single or married, having great sex or no sex, your sexuality is inseparable from your spirituality. In fact, every sexual choice is also a spiritual choice. Sex isn't just about sex.

Take a moment to digest that. Most Christian women have built a thick wall between their sexuality and spirituality. Their sexual fantasies, sexual shame, and temptations are far removed from their desire to please and know the Lord. I believe that the walls we build between the sexual and spiritual are only imaginary. Confusion and hidden pain related to sex is intricately intertwined with our present relationship with God.

John Piper wrote, "The ultimate reason (not the only reason) why we are sexual is to make God more deeply knowable."[2]

What do you think of the above quote? Kind of a paradigm shift, isn't it? God created sex for a lot of reasons—for procreation, for pleasure, for intimate knowing between a husband and wife. However, one of the most important reasons He created sex is to communicate about Himself.

God understands that we are limited creatures—that we have difficulty grasping spiritual truths. All throughout Scripture, God paints physical pictures to explain spiritual truths. For example, in John 15, He used the physical picture of a grapevine to explain what looks like to abide in Christ. God even tells us to *do* physical things (like take communion) in order to *remem-*

*ber* spiritual truths (like Jesus' sacrifice for our sins).

God created sex and the covenant of marriage to be a brilliant metaphor of how deeply He knows us and longs for us to know Him. It's not just John Piper who says this. Consider this fact. The Hebrew word for sexual intimacy between a husband and wife in the Old Testament is the word *yada,* which literally means, "to know deeply or intimately." The word *yada* appears in the Old Testament over 940 times. No, there isn't that much sex in the Old Testament. The word *yada* is most often used to describe intimacy with God—His with us, and ours with Him. Here are a few examples:

> You have searched me, Lord, and you *yada* me.
> (Psalm 139:1)
> In all your ways *yada* him and he will make your paths straight." (Proverbs 3:6)
> Moses said to the Lord . . . "If you are pleased with me, teach me your ways so I may *yada* you and continue to find favor with you." (Exodus 33:12–13)

Sexual intimacy is a powerful picture of the gospel—of the degree of intimacy and ecstasy we are capable of having with God. The Christian marriage is designed to showcase this masterpiece. The promise of marriage (till death do us part) is an echo of God's covenant love, "I will never leave you or forsake you." The romantic longings of a single woman mirror the longings of a bride who is waiting for the ultimate salvation—the coming of Jesus Christ. To the extent that our understanding and experience of sexuality is damaged and twisted, our view of God is compromised.

Your sexuality isn't just about what you choose to do with your body. It's about living out a holy metaphor within the messiness of a fallen and broken world.

Here's the takeaway: What you think about sex really matters. Having God's perspective on the topic, whether you are single or married, is a vital piece of your growth as a daughter of God.

### *A call to sexual discipleship*

My guess is that you probably haven't seen those two words together. What is sexual discipleship? Our approach to sexuality is often compartmentalized. A loving parent has the "sex talk" with her son or daughter in adolescence. Maybe once a year the pastor mentions the importance of sexual purity. But our understanding of sex is rarely integrated with the rest of who we are as Christ-followers.

The result of this is that Christians often commit their lives to Christ but reserve their sexuality for themselves. There are men and women who have left everything and moved to the mission field, yet continue to exercise their sexuality according to their own desire. A godly wife insists, "It's my body—my right. I don't owe my husband anything in the bedroom." Others study at Bible college to prepare for full-time ministry while sleeping around or looking at porn.

One reason for this disconnect is that we don't have a practical theology of sex. Most of us don't have a clue how much worldly teaching has infiltrated our thinking about sex. Throughout a lifetime in the Western world, we will be bombarded with millions of messages and examples exalting sexual immorality. Although the Bible has a lot to say about sex, we rarely hear this message.

Hudson Taylor wrote, "If God is not Lord *of* all, He is not Lord *at* all."[3] Let me ask you a personal question. Is God Lord of your sexuality? If someone were to look solely at your sexuality, would there be evidence that Jesus Christ is your Savior and Lord?

A follower of Christ intentionally sets his or her mind on what the Spirit desires, not what the flesh demands. Sexual discipleship means that you are willing to yield this very personal and vulnerable area of your life completely to the Lord, trusting that His ways are good.

Throughout this book, we will be tackling some very practical questions about sex. My hope is that the Lord will reveal how we can surrender even this most intimate area of our lives to Him. As God brings His truth and healing into your heart, may you grow closer to Him in *all* areas of your life. Thanks for joining me on this journey!

WHO are YOU
to JUDGE
MY SEXUAL
CHOICES?

## 2

Okay. Let me just put it out there. As we wade through the waters of women's most common questions about sex, we may step on some toes. We're not going to get very far in this book before something you read seems offensive and even judgmental. After all, you can't address cohabitation, erotica, masturbation, and homosexuality without ruffling some feathers. I will take a moral stand within the perspectives I offer on these topics. Why? Because I truly believe that God designed sexuality, and He knows a lot more about it than anyone else does. I also believe that God is loving when He says "no" to something, it is ultimately for our benefit.

I have the advantage as a psychologist to see this truth play out in real life. There are consequences when we violate God's standard. As common as they have become, divorce, sexual abuse, "hooking up," abortion, and adultery always leave pain in their wake. The idea of "free love" and everyone making up their own morality has led to bondage, not freedom. Depression, addictions, and almost every other psychological disorder are on the rise, not the decline, and the prevailing attitudes of moral relativism are partly to blame. It's time to admit that our experiment with "anything goes" sexuality isn't bringing us happiness in the long run.

Many Christians living in this postmodern world just want to keep their mouths shut instead of taking a moral stand on sexual ethics. They fear being perceived as offensive or unloving. But what would you think of a doctor who, in the spirit of being nonjudgmental, won't tell his obese patient that his lifestyle could kill him? Or an accountant who hates confrontation and so doesn't warn her clients that they are violating the tax code?

The most unloving thing I could do throughout this book is to withhold the truth about God's design for sex. By sharing my beliefs, I am not telling you what to choose for your own life. That is between you and God. But please understand that sharing biblical truth is NOT the same as judging. Here are a few key reasons why.

### *Sharing a biblical perspective is appealing to a moral authority.*

Throughout hundreds of generations, the Bible has been viewed as the trusted authority of truth and morality. Jews, Christians, and even many governments use the Judeo-Christian ethic expressed in the Bible (like the Ten Commandments) as the basis for moral understanding. To fear the Lord is the beginning of wisdom. While many people today want to chuck the Bible and embrace relativism, it is not judgmental or arrogant to hold to God's Word as a moral standard. In fact, we could argue the arrogance of relying on "what seems right to me" instead of trusting that our Creator has expressed His will for us regarding right and wrong.

But in today's culture, right and wrong are sorted through a grid of how *we* think, how *we* understand life, and what *we* perceive as being the best for ourselves and our fellow humans. Essentially, human beings are gods with the authority to determine our own moral compass.

From this worldview, morality is defined as "do no harm." Ethics and morality are measured by whether or not people are hurt. "She's not hurting anyone, so how could she be doing something wrong?"

Can something be immoral even if it doesn't "hurt" someone else? Up until a few decades ago, we considered ourselves a "God-fearing" society. Even those who didn't claim to be Christians had a sense of honoring God as a moral authority. Consensual sex outside of marriage, visiting strip clubs, and swearing were immoral even though they didn't "harm" others. Morality was based on God's expressed design for how and why He created humanity. Now it seems like everything is okay as long as no one gets hurt. This is humanism at its finest. Even God exists only if He suits our purposes. Paul predicted that we would be exactly in this place (see 2 Timothy 3).

If you are a follower of the Lord, you can't base moral decisions *primarily* on how those decisions affect other people. A biblical definition of right and wrong is based first and foremost on honoring and revering God. Before Jesus told us to "love your neighbors as yourself," He said that the greatest command was to "love the Lord your God with all your heart and with all your soul and with all your mind and with all your strength." Even more important than how we treat each other is the complete surrender to and worship of our Creator. We have no greater call on our lives than to submit to His will and His design.

The thoughts in this book are about more than my personal opinions or experiences. I'm not the one who decided that sleeping around is morally wrong. Actually, my opinion on the topic isn't worth a whole lot. Anything I say or teach needs to come from a source much more trustworthy than my experiences and conclusions.

If there is no God, our cultural values are correct—everyone should do what is right in their own eyes. But if there is a God, we must worship Him and submit to His will as revealed in the Bible. He is the only one who has the authority to define morality, "for there is no authority except from God, and those which exist are established by God" (Romans 13:1 NASB).

### I'm just as accountable to these standards as you are.

When confronted with a Christian sexual ethic, people love to quote Jesus' words, "Do not judge, or you too will be judged" (Matthew 7:1). Right after this statement, Jesus explains that we must first take the log out of our own eye before we can see clearly to take the speck of dust out of our brother's eye. In other words, none of us are ready to make a proper judgment until we have asked God to search our own hearts. This is where we often fall into hypocritically judging other people. We look at their sexual sin as far more serious than our own rationalized "shortcomings."

Perhaps this is one reason why there is so much pushback against evangelical statements about homosexuality. Christians quote Romans 1 as evidence that the gay lifestyle is immoral. What they often fail to do is apply the first few verses of Romans 2 in that discussion. Paul writes,

> You, therefore, have no excuse, you who pass judgment on someone else, for at whatever point you judge another, you are condemning yourself, because you who pass judgments do the same things. Now we know that God's judgment against those who do such things is based on truth. So when you, a mere human being, pass judgment on them and yet do the same things, do you think you will escape God's judgment? (Romans 2:1–3)

Many people hear a Christian's perspective of morality and write it off, viewing the church as a group of hypocrites. Divorce, adultery, porn, cheating, sexual abuse, lying, gossip, pride—they are all rampant among those who call themselves Christians. Instead of admitting our sin, we rationalize it. Such hypocrisy will always water down the impact of God's truth, but it doesn't change the truth itself.

I recently was devastated to learn that one of my favorite Bible teachers was involved in ongoing sexual immorality. This man's sermons had greatly impacted me. Yet while he was teaching those very sermons, he was sexually unfaithful to his wife. His immoral behavior did not invalidate the truths he was teaching, but disqualified him as a messenger. *The pride and immorality of Christians doesn't erase God's moral standard or pending judgment. They only cripple us as messengers of that truth.*

Biblical statements that tell us not to judge are not suggesting that we throw away God's standard of right and wrong. The purpose of these passages is to remind us that we are in need of God's grace as much as anyone! I am subject to every word I teach. In fact, James says that not many people should be teachers because those who teach God's Word will be held to an even higher standard.

### *There is a difference between evangelism and discipleship.*

One of the worst ways of telling someone about God is to point out the sin in their life. Christians often make the mistake of blaming the world for living like the world. In the book of Romans, Paul wrote that people who don't know God are literally enslaved to their own desires. In other words, it shouldn't be a surprise when people who don't know God make reckless moral and sexual choices. Paul says as much in 1 Corinthians

5:12–13, "What business is it of mine to judge those outside the church? Are you not to judge those inside? God will judge those outside."

What should surprise us is when Christians who claim to follow Christ disregard biblical teaching on morality and sexuality. Paul wrote to the Thessalonian church, "It is God's will that you should be sanctified: that you should avoid sexual immorality; that each of you should learn to control your own body in a way that is holy and honorable, not in passionate lust like the pagans who do not know God" (1 Thessalonians 4:3–5).

Let me ask you a personal question. Are you a seeker or are you a follower? Have you committed your life to Christ and trusted Him for salvation? Or are you still investigating this "Christian" thing? If you have not made the decision to put your faith in Jesus Christ, what the Bible says about sex may mean very little to you. In fact, it may offend you to learn that your choices are considered immoral.

Jesus encountered many men and women when He lived on this earth. His first words to them were not condemnation, but an invitation—an invitation to forgiveness, trust, eternal life, and intimacy with Him. Please don't miss that invitation because you are so focused on what is sin and what isn't. The truth is that all of us have sinned and are worthy of condemnation. But Jesus died to take the punishment for our sin and to invite us into a new life. You don't have to "clean up your act" before you come to Jesus. He will meet you where you are and give you the wisdom and strength to live a life according to His will for you.

While many "seekers" are offended by the concept of moral absolutes, unfortunately many Christians don't take biblical teaching on sexuality seriously either. If you fall into this category, God's words are more of a rebuke than an invitation:

"Run from sexual sin! No other sin so clearly affects the body as this one does. For sexual immorality is a sin against your own body. Don't you realize that your body is the temple of the Holy Spirit, who lives in you and was given to you by God? You do not belong to yourself, for God bought you with a high price. So you must honor God with your body" (1 Corinthians 6:18–20 NLT).

The Christian life isn't just about choosing a particular religion or moral code. It is about the death and resurrection of Jesus Christ absolutely transforming our lives. Throughout this book, every question will be viewed in the light of "how do I glorify God through my sexuality?"

The underlying truth I want to share in this book is that God has a bigger "yes" for you. God is actually *for* great sex within the right context. He has created us as sexual creatures and designed our sexuality to be a blessing, not a source of condemnation.

Can I be SINGLE -and- SEXUAL?

# 3

Did you know that single women are sexual? That your sexuality has nothing to do with whether or not you are having sex? As ridiculous as it sounds, many Christians grow up thinking that they will magically become sexual when they get married. It's as if the pronouncement of the vows and the golden band placed on the ring finger somehow makes you a sexual person. Before the big day, you aren't supposed to even have a sexual thought.

Singles are sexual beings created in the image of God. Your sexuality is not compartmentalized, waiting for marriage; it's integrated into all the aspects of your being—intellectual, emotional, relational, and spiritual. It's a core part of who God created you to be.

I deeply believe that the biblical teaching to reserve sexual intimacy for marriage is still relevant for today's Christian woman. The fullness of sexual expression was created to be expressed only within the covenant of marriage. No amount of modern science or situational ethics can erase the fact that your sexuality is about more than your body. Sexual intercourse is a powerful emotional and spiritual bonding that will always have implications; there is no such thing as "casual sex."

But while God commands you to save sexual intimacy for marriage, your sexuality is something that is always there, even when sex isn't a part of your life. Because we tend to talk only about the physical *act* of sex, we ignore the fact that it's our sexuality that ultimately drives us into relationship, makes us desire marriage, expresses our longing to be known, heard, understood, and protected—our longing to be vulnerable, soul to soul, with another person, and ultimately, our longing to be known by God. As a single person, your sexuality serves a purpose.

### *Sexuality draws us into relationship.*

I was recently talking with a woman in her thirties who had lived a season of life as bisexual. Over the past few years, she became convicted that her sexual relationships were not what God wanted for her life. Yet she was still confused about what that meant.

"Juli, I still really want to be close with women. I love my friends and hate the fact that I can't be intimate with them." As we talked, I helped this young woman unravel the concepts of intimacy and sex. In our world, the two ideas have become intertwined. In fact, sexual intimacy is just one aspect of intimacy.

I have intimate relationships with men and women, but I am not having sex with them.

A core aspect of our sexuality is the yearning to be known and to share intimately with another person. Yes, that is expressed in its fullness in marriage. Yet, my sexuality as a woman deeply impacts how I relate to others outside the bedroom. Your longing to nurture, to connect, to share, and to trust another person wholly are all aspects of God's image expressed in your femininity and sexuality.

### Sexuality teaches us about God

Ephesians 5:31–32 alludes to the fact that sex within marriage is a holy metaphor that points to the spiritual mystery of God's covenant love for us. Throughout Scripture, sex is used to express aspects of God's covenant and the degree of intimacy He has with His people. This means that married men and women should be learning mysteries of God as they experience sex together. I believe singles can also understand something deeper about God through their sexuality. Jesus talked about how we will mourn and long for the Bridegroom when He is not with us. We will ache for His presence and have deep longings that are unmet. Singles definitely get this!

When I read the expressions of spiritual longing expressed in some of the Psalms, I can't help but think of a single woman yearning for true intimacy. Here are a few examples:

O God, you are my God; I earnestly search for you. My soul thirsts for you; my whole body longs for you in this parched and weary land where there is no water (Psalm 63:1).
My soul yearns, even faints, for the courts of the Lord; my heart and my flesh cry out for the living God (Psalm 84:2).

### *The struggle for sexual purity isn't just for singles.*

Married and single women have a lot more in common than they realize. I think we do each other a great disservice when we compartmentalize sexual conversations to single and married women. Do you know that many married women struggle with sexual frustration and temptations?

I've met with young men and women who think that their struggle to stay pure will end with a wedding ceremony. Wrong! Sexual purity is a battle throughout adulthood. It simply takes a different form in marriage. Your married friends are free to have sex, but that doesn't mean they aren't struggling with porn, unmet desires, images from the past, extramarital flirtations, and conflict over sex in marriage.

Why is this important for you to know as a single? Because it helps you understand that your sexuality is not about an "on-off" switch called marriage. It means understanding that being an adult sexual woman is part of God's design for you as one who bears the image of Christ. I don't fully understand it—it's a mystery, but it's still a reality.

Single or married, yielding your sexuality under the Lordship of Christ will always be a challenge. In this season of singleness, it doesn't help to pretend that you aren't sexual. Instead, how can you express your sexuality in ways that are honoring to God and that validate your longings for intimacy? Here are a few thoughts:

### Guard your mind

We live in a culture that is sex-saturated. For many, the accessibility of porn on every mobile device makes it seem impossible to not think about sex. Other women aren't tempted by visual porn, but allow themselves to consume "emotional porn"—movies, romance novels, and reality shows that present romance in a light far from reality.

Song of Songs warns us not to awaken love before its time (2:7; also 3:5). You need to know what fuels your reactions—and protect yourself accordingly.

### Channel your desire for intimacy in healthy ways

Remember that intimacy doesn't mean sex. Show me a woman who is hooked on *Fifty Shades of Grey,* and I'll show you a woman who is lonely. She's longing for intimacy—the feeling of being known, cherished, valued, and loved.

But no amount of sex (real or imagined) can compensate for a lack of intimacy.

While God may or may not have marriage for you in the future, His will for you is to have intimate relationships within the body of Christ. In some cases, deep friendships can be even more fulfilling than marriage. David expressed this about his intimate friendship with Jonathan: "The soul of Jonathan was knit to the soul of David, and Jonathan loved him as his own soul" (1 Samuel 18:1 ESV). Paul, who was single most (if not all) of his life, often speaks lovingly in his letters about many intimate friendships that encouraged him through the years.

### *Take a lesson from a widow*

The other day, I noticed an "unsung heroine" among the women of the Bible. Her name was Anna. We don't know much about her, but here is her testimony recorded in Luke:

> There was also a prophet, Anna, the daughter of Phanuel, of the tribe of Asher. She was very old; she had lived with her husband seven years after her marriage, and then was a widow until she was eighty-four. She never left the temple but worshiped night and day, fasting and praying. Coming up to them at that very moment, she gave thanks to God and spoke about the child to all who were looking forward to the redemption of Jerusalem. (Luke 2:36–38)

Here was a widow who knew marital and sexual intimacy as a young woman. When she was widowed, she didn't search for intimacy in another man, but by seeking the Lord until she was eighty-four years old. Her constant pursuit was rewarded with the presence of the living Messiah!

If Anna were alive today, I wonder what her advice would be. I'd love to ask her about her experience as a married woman who then chose a life of singleness, seeking intimacy with God. We so often view "intimacy with God" as a trite suggestion for our loneliness. Yet, Anna was a woman who believed that worshiping and seeking God could be even more fulfilling than the expression of her sexuality in marriage.

Does this mean that we should all become nuns and be "married to Christ"? No. As Paul taught in 1 Corinthians 7, we each have different callings. Some women serve the Lord as wives and moms. However, there is true intimacy to be found in worship and obedience to the Lord. You may sing about it every Sunday, but have you experienced it? Do you know what it is to cry out as David did, "My heart and my flesh cry out for the living God" (Psalm 84:2)? He will answer.

While marriage is a wonderful thing to seek, intimacy is the greater goal. Allow your sexuality and your longings to remind you that God has created you for relationship—relationship with others and with Him.

Is it
WRONG
~~~~~
to
LIKE SEX?

# 4

It may seem weird to see the words *God* and *sex* in the same sentence. Sometimes when I teach women on this topic, they have a visceral reaction to the concept of God knowing about their sex life. Psalm 139 tells us that God is always with us. There is nowhere we can go to hide from His presence—not even the bedroom!

Why is it so hard for many of us to grasp the idea that God cares about our sex life? When I probe past the initial "That's just weird!" reaction, I see that most women view sex as earthy, dirty, and shameful—everything that God is not. Inviting God into the bedroom seems as absurd as asking a Boston Red Sox fan to dress in a Yankees uniform. The two seem absolutely incompatible.

Many women learned about sexual pleasure through a shameful experience. Hardly a week goes by that I don't get a question like this one,

Hi, Dr. Slattery. I need your advice related to my two-year-old daughter. It's embarrassing to admit it, but I sometimes find her touching herself. She most often does it at night or when she's sleepy. My husband and I have told her to stop, slapped her hand away and used other punishments, but she keeps doing it. How can I get her to stop?

Why do loving mothers like this one automatically think of smacking their toddler's hand away in this situation? Why is touching your genitals, even as a young child, considered shameful? Young children naturally repeat whatever feels soothing and pleasurable. They suck their thumbs, pick their noses, and twirl their hair. Over time, they learn appropriate boundaries for what is acceptable behavior.

You may be surprised to find that there is nothing in the Bible that supports the assumption that sexual pleasure is innately dirty, shameful, and sinful. That may be Christian tradition, but it certainly isn't biblical. God equipped both male and female bodies with the capacity to experience great pleasure through sexual touching and expression. He placed the greatest concentration of nerve endings in both the male and female genitalia. There is nothing inherently wrong with the pleasure that comes from sexual touch.

What makes sexual pleasure right or wrong is how we pursue it. While a young child doesn't know the moral implications of her various body parts, as adults we understand that God has called us to honor Him with how we exercise our sexuality.

Proverbs chapter 5 tells us all we need to know about sexual pleasure. Outside of marriage, pursuing sexual pleasure is a dangerous pursuit. In fact, it can lead to death—the death of a ministry, a marriage, a testimony, of intimacy with God.

In this Proverb, Solomon presents a clear picture of the consequences of sexual immorality. Having sex with someone you are not married to or looking at pornographic pictures of a stranger is not only immoral, but also hazardous to your own emotional and spiritual health. Just think of how many lives you know that have been ruined by impulsive sexual behavior. The wisdom of Proverbs tells men and women to flee from sexual temptation. It is powerful and deadly.

My son, pay attention to my wisdom, turn your ear to my words of insight, that you may maintain discretion and your lips may preserve knowledge. For the lips of the adulterous woman drip honey, and her speech is smoother than oil; but in the end she is bitter as gall, sharp as a double-edged sword. Her feet go down to death; her steps lead straight to the grave. She gives no thought to the way of life; her paths wander aimlessly, but she does not know it. Now then, my sons, listen to me; do not turn aside from what I say. Keep to a path far from her, do not go near the door of her house, lest you lose your honor to others and your dignity to one who is cruel, lest strangers feast on your wealth and your toil enrich the house of another. At the end of your life you will groan, when your flesh and body are spent.

These verses in Proverbs 51:–11 probably don't surprise you. If you've grown up in the church, you know the warnings about sexual immorality. What comes next, however, may surprise you. There is an abrupt change in the passage:

> Let your fountain be blessed, and rejoice in the wife of your youth, a lovely deer, a graceful doe. Let her breasts fill you at all times with delight; be intoxicated always in her love. (Proverbs 5:18–19 ESV)

All of a sudden, sexual pleasure has become a wonderful, God-given gift. A husband is told to always delight in the sexual love of his wife. Wives are to do the same.

The entire Song of Songs validates the message of Proverbs 5:15–19. Within the covenant of marriage, erotic, exciting sex is a worthy pursuit for both the husband and the wife. The apostle Paul taught that a godly marriage should include frequent and satisfying sexual intimacy (1 Corinthians 7:3–5).

Men and particularly women struggle to make the shift between Proverbs 5:14 and 15. After years of warnings like "don't give yourself away, don't think about sex, sex is bad!" all of a sudden, a wedding ceremony transforms erotic pleasure into something holy and honoring to God.

However . . . a wedding ring doesn't somehow redeem your sexual drive. Your body was created to be sexual and to experience sexual pleasure as part of the image of God. Your sexual drive speaks to the innate, God-given passion to connect, commit, celebrate, and share yourself in the most intimate way with another human being. While sexual restraint is the challenge *before* marriage, uninhibited sexual expression may be a challenge *within* marriage.

Somehow, many Christians believe it honors God to withhold or subdue sexual pleasure in the marriage bed. Nothing could be further from the truth! Within the covenant of marriage, you have God's permission to throw off every restraint and enjoy to the fullest the gift of sexual expression with your spouse.

In the Bible study *Passion Pursuit: What Kind of Love Are You Making?* Linda Dillow and I suggest that God has given a married couple a "permission slip."[1] In other words, He tells a husband and wife, "You have My complete blessing to enjoy this gift I have given you." Unfortunately, many married women don't know how to accept that permission slip. Sometimes because of past wounds or mistakes they feel guilty about, women withhold pleasure from themselves. Other women simply can't figure out *how* to enjoy sex. And still others subconsciously hold on to the message that sexual pleasure is shameful.

It has been quite a journey for me to embrace sexual pleasure in my own marriage. I had many barriers to overcome, including physical pain and confusion about God's view of sex. I didn't aggressively pursue healing in these areas until I understood that it actually pleases the Lord for a married couple to enjoy erotic pleasure together.

As a married woman, withholding sexual pleasure from yourself or your husband is not a God-honoring endeavor. In fact, you have the opportunity to redeem the beautiful gift of erotic love from the many ways in which it has been distorted in our world. Have you accepted the "permission slip" to enjoy sex in your marriage?

and
I WAITED
→ for ←
THIS?

# 5

Several months ago, a young woman wrote a blog about sexual purity that went viral.[1] As a former Christian, her primary thesis was that saving herself for marriage was one of the worst mistakes she ever made. After years of virginity, her honeymoon was a disaster—and things didn't get better in the first two years of marriage.

"[Waiting for marriage] controlled my identity for over a decade, landed me in therapy, and left me a stranger in my own skin. I was so completely ashamed of my body and my sexuality that it made having sex a demoralizing experience."

This woman's sexual experience after waiting for marriage not only changed her views on sexual purity, it completely altered her worldview.

"I don't go to church anymore, nor am I religious. As I started to heal, I realized that I couldn't figure out how to be both religious and sexual at the same time. I chose sex. Every single day is a battle to remember that my body belongs to me and not to the church of my childhood."

Oh, how I wish I could have talked to this dear woman in the midst of her struggle to make sense of sexual frustration! Her statements represent many young wives who are deeply disappointed at the realities of sexuality, particularly after decades of "waiting." Her pain raises the question: Are we setting young women up for unhappiness and failure by telling them that sex is worth waiting for?

Now that my honeymoon is over twenty years in the rearview mirror, I can more openly share that the first several years of intimacy in my marriage were less than satisfying. I remember hearing that sex was a gift. Once I opened it, I was looking for a way to return it. It's not that I didn't like sex; it's that intercourse actually hurt for many years. I resented the fact my husband's favorite activity had to come at the expense of my pain. Some gift!

Instead of concluding that sex was going to be a continual disappointment, I wanted to understand God's design for sex in my marriage—a design that had to include the obstacles Mike and I were experiencing. What I've learned is that the gift of sex is a lot more complicated than I once thought. I've learned to think about sex as a gift like Legos.

The first time a kid sees a box of Legos, he *might* be naïve enough to think that the box actually contains a toy that looks like the cool picture on the front. Imagine his disappointment when he opens the Legos to find hundreds of seemingly random pieces of plastic instead of the Batmobile or Starship that was promised by the box cover.

The genius and fun of Legos is creativity. First, you follow the directions and build the design represented on the box. But then no child can resist the desire to build something new, to tear the blocks apart and start another creation.

Back to sex . . . Your church youth group may have painted for you a picture on the box—a blissful experience of exquisite pleasure and oneness after years of waiting. Perhaps you have been surprised and disappointed to find that sex has created more conflict in your marriage than intimacy, more pain than pleasure. The metaphoric "pieces" of this gift seem to be strewn around your bedroom, bearing no semblance to the gift you were promised.

Every marriage experiences some obstacle to physical intimacy. Differences in desire, medical issues, recovery from sexual abuse, baggage from poor choices in the past, involvement with porn, a poor body image, or (like the blogger) unbalanced Christian teaching can all set a couple up for sexual disappointment. I'm sure you've had periods of your marriage, as I have, in which you ask God, "Wasn't this supposed to be a gift? With all due respect, God, I think the gift is broken. Any chance I can exchange it for something else?"

What we don't realize is that God can use the frustration as part of the gift. Sexual intimacy isn't just a means of expressing love. Nor is it primarily a way to feel close. Sex is also the laboratory in which our love is tested, revealed, and refined.

While I strongly believe that waiting for marriage is the right thing, I also think we can set young men and women up for disappointment when we give them a simplistic view of sex and marriage. "Just wait for marriage and your sex life will be amazing!" The joys of intimacy in marriage can be wonderful but it often doesn't start out that way. A great sex life (and a great marriage, for that matter) takes work.

For most couples the bedroom initially causes frustration and friction rather than elation. That doesn't mean they are sexually incompatible. It means they have just opened the "Lego box." Now it's time to start learning to build.

What no one told me was that the honeymoon was just the beginning of the journey. We were just getting started. I also didn't understand that the greatest benefits from sex would not be the experience itself, but what happens throughout the journey of learning to love each other. If sex had been easy for us, I don't think Mike and I would have the intimacy we have today. The struggles and disappointments caused us to seek God, be honest about very vulnerable things, and extend mercy to each other.

If you are disappointed with sex in your marriage, please consider that sex is like Legos. You are just beginning to build, and it will get better if you pursue God's true design. Sometimes "building" intimacy means seeking professional help from a doctor or counselor.

Also remember that God never wastes our pain. He can use the very things that cause you frustration to teach you about how to really love each other.

# WHY do GUYS CARE SO MUCH — about — SEX?

# 6

Author Robert Byrne once said, "Anyone who believes that the way to a man's heart is through his stomach flunked anatomy."[2] For most men, the pathway to the greatest pleasure is through another organ. We joke about it and complain about it, but few women understand why sex is such a priority for men. For the average woman, sex is a nice addition to a good marriage relationship. During times of busyness, stress, and conflict, most wives are happy to put sexual intimacy on the back burner. Not so for most husbands. About 70–80 percent of men rate sex as the most important aspect of marriage for them. When sex is absent or unfulfilling, it is a big deal.

Before going any further, I want to acknowledge that in some marriages, sex doesn't seem like a priority to a husband. Maybe you want sex more often than your husband does. Even if this is the case, it doesn't discount the fact that sex is still a significant aspect of your man's life. Your husband's sexuality is integrated into his masculinity whether or not he has a high sex drive. If this dynamic describes your marriage, make sure you check out the next question, "What if I want sex more than my husband does?"

Many women view a guy's sexual desire as indication that he is a Neanderthal of some sort. "Why does he *always* want sex? It seems to be his solution to every conflict or stress in our marriage!" Women think it is more mature to work on emotional or spiritual intimacy than to put such a priority on sex. What we often don't understand is that sex isn't just about sex. Yes, the physical release and pleasure are a key part of sex, but sex also has emotional and spiritual implications.

It has taken me years as a wife to understand that my husband's sex drive is actually a wonderful gift to me in our marriage. It is a primary way that I can connect to him, not just physically, but emotionally and spiritually as well. If that concept just piled on a heap of guilt, keep reading.

Although the average wife may acknowledge that her husband's sex drive is stronger than hers, she probably still underestimates the impact of sex on their relationship. According to a poll of 150 Christian married men, 83 percent stated that they don't believe that women understand a man's sex drive.[3] Most guys don't even attempt to communicate with their wives about sex, assuming that she won't understand.

Wives are continually bombarded with the message "Your husband needs sex, so give it to him." I've met many women who feel an incredible amount of pressure to meet their husband's sexual desires, even at the expense of their own discomfort or pain. I've met many others who carry constant guilt for not having sex more often, knowing how important it is to their husband. To make matters more complicated, guys really don't enjoy sex when it's approached as a household duty, so a wife doesn't just need to be willing, she also has to find a way to enjoy it. Now that's pressure—so much pressure that some women pretend to enjoy it when they really don't!

Although it doesn't solve every problem in the bedroom, understanding why sex is such an important aspect of marriage for a guy may change your paradigm of how you approach your husband sexually.

### *Understanding the physical drive*

One of the biggest differences between you and your husband is that he will experience sex as a pressing physical urge. Let me clarify—not a need, but an urge. No man has ever died from a lack of sex. However, the desire for sex for a man has a physiological element. His level of sexual desire is determined by many different factors, including his environment, but the primary influence is the amount of testosterone in his body.

The physical urge for sexual release intensifies as sperm builds in the testicles. The body continues to produce and store sperm, although sperm production fluctuates based on testosterone and the frequency of sexual release. Right after a sexual release, men are physically satisfied. As time goes on, sexual thoughts again become more prevalent and are more easily aroused.

The best way for a woman to understand this dynamic is to relate it to something that we have experienced. If you've had a baby, you probably remember the pressure of milk building up in your breasts a few days after giving birth. The buildup becomes annoying—even painful—until the milk is expressed. Just as with breast milk, sperm production tends to "keep up with demand." The more often a man has sex, the more semen his body will produce. The buildup of semen doesn't mean that a man *has* to have sex. However, sexual thoughts and desires become more predominant.

As women, we don't tend to experience the physical drive for sex in this same way. Rather than a "buildup" that demands release, the fluctuation of hormones drives our sexuality.

### *Understanding the emotional connection*

Men can experience sexual arousal apart from emotional connection. However, that doesn't mean that sex isn't also a relational and emotional aspect of a man's life. God never intended for a man's sexuality to be separate from the rest of his life.

When my husband and I haven't connected in a few days, the last thing I want to do is have sex. His approach, however, is quite different. "It's how I feel close to you," Mike says.

As our understanding of brain chemistry has expanded, we now know that sex really is the way that most husbands feel connected to their wives.

Having sex in marriage releases important hormones in the

male brain, including dopamine (the "feel good" hormone) and oxytocin (the bonding hormone). In fact, a man who has regular sex with his wife can actually become "addicted" to her. The word *addiction* always has a negative connotation in our minds. In essence, we become addicted to harmful things like drugs and pornography when we pair these potent brain responses inappropriately, but there are also "healthy addictions" to things like human contact, exercise, and sex in marriage. God has a purpose in how He created sexuality to produce a powerful response in a man. It's a wonderful thing when a man learns to find his greatest pleasure through intimacy with his wife!

When a man has an orgasm, the release of these brain chemicals can trigger an intoxicating effect in which he views his wife as more beautiful and desirable than he would without sex. After more than twenty years of marriage, I think it's amazing that my husband still likes to look at my naked body—not because I'm gorgeous but because his brain has been trained to find me desirable.

Do you want your husband to pay attention to you? Have you been trying to get him to communicate, go to marriage seminars, or read a marriage book? If you really want his attention, work with the way God designed him. A great sex life won't solve the problems in your marriage. However, it will ramp up your husband's affection and attraction to you, and this can be key to working on issues like communication, conflict resolution, and building emotional intimacy.

## *Understanding the spiritual need*

We've already addressed the fact that sex is a spiritual meta-phor and that our sexual choices impact our spiritual lives. For a man, this often plays out in the area of his sexual integrity.

Most men have a daily battle to stay sexually pure. Your hus-band's walk with the Lord and his integrity are largely deter-mined by how he channels sexual urges and temptations. There are many godly men (and women) who carry tremendous guilt because of battles with porn or other immoral behaviors.

Archibald Hart explains a man's struggle for sexual integrity like this: "Most men face a lifelong struggle to control their sex-uality. The struggle is between their hormones and their higher aspirations. It is a battle between the seemingly uncontrollable urges and the fear of succumbing to these urges. Ultimately, it is a struggle over integrity, right and wrong, uprightness and wholeness."[4]

In this letter to the early church, Paul got pretty practical about what to do if a man is sexually tempted:

Since sexual immorality is occurring, each man should have sexual relations with his own wife, and each woman with her own husband. The husband should fulfill his marital duty to his wife, and likewise the wife to her husband. The wife does not have authority over her own body but yields it to her husband. In the same way, the husband does not have authority over his own body but yields it to his wife. Do not deprive each other except perhaps by mutual consent and for a time, so that you may devote yourselves to prayer. Then come together again so that Satan will not tempt you because of your lack of self-control (1 Corinthians 7:2–5).

Paul is stating here that one of the most important ways to stay sexually pure is to get married and to have regular sex within marriage. As a wife, think of it this way. The only holy sexual outlet you and your husband have is enjoying each other. Any other sexual expression leads to sin. Marriage means that a man shouldn't have to fight temptation alone. He has a partner to share the emotional, physical, and spiritual aspects of his sexuality with.

Please understand that no wife is responsible for her husband's sexual choices. Even a man whose wife withholds sex doesn't have an excuse to seek sexual pleasure outside of his marriage. However, a wife has a lot of power to be an encouragement to her husband sexually. Although you aren't responsible for his actions, you are a key component to his victory. You are the only woman in the world who your husband can look at sexually without compromising his integrity. That's a lot of power!

Meeting your husband's sexual needs is about much more than giving him your body. It means inviting his sexuality into your marriage, embracing all that he is as a sexual person. It includes wanting to fully understand him and validating the sexual appetite that expresses his masculinity.

What if
I WANT SEX
more than
MY HUSBAND
does?

# 7

I get asked this a lot. The woman often sheepishly approaches me at an event and says, "I'm one of those women you talked about who has a higher sex drive than my husband. What should I do?"

Because women in this situation defy the stereotype, they sometimes feel shame and inadequacy. *I must not be pretty or sexy enough. Is there something wrong with me?*

For many women, the "men always want sex" stereotype has been fed to them for so many years that they assume their husband will always be initiating and constantly in the mood. When he isn't, they sit silently and make a list of all the things that must be wrong with them. STOP!

Practically every couple has difficulties to overcome in their sexual relationship. Each husband and wife has their own unique set of strengths, weaknesses, and areas of incompatibility. If this is something you're struggling with, please don't add to it by assuming there must be something wrong with you.

Despite what you might have picked up in Christian circles, there is nothing in the Bible that says that a husband should or does have a higher sex drive than his wife. In fact, the Bible assumes that both the husband and wife have sexual needs. First Corinthians 7 records Paul's teaching that many use to promote a "wifely duty." Here is the passage:

The husband should fulfill his marital duty to his wife, and likewise the wife to her husband. The wife does not have authority over her own body but yields it to her husband. In the same way, the husband does not have authority over his own body but yields it to his wife. Do not deprive each other except perhaps by mutual consent and for a time, so that you may devote yourselves to prayer (1 Corinthians 7:3–5a).

Did you notice that a "husbandly duty" is mentioned even before the "wifely duty"? Interesting, huh? Even in Paul's day there were probably women who were frustrated by the lack of sex in their marriage.

### *Start with a conversation*

Have you and your husband talked about this issue? Because these are such sensitive topics, many couples only address sexual differences when they are fighting. Instead of talking, they settle into patterns that lead to rejection and frustration. You initiate or hint toward intimacy and he turns you down. You get angry and lash out or avoid him. This kind of pattern becomes ingrained until even the mention of sex becomes a powder keg. Both husband and wife feel misunderstood and marginalized. You will never solve the problem until you learn to talk about it with the goal of understanding each other and getting on the same team.

One of the first things to do is start a conversation with your spouse and not assume the worst. One wife put it like this:

> I would count how many nights in a row we weren't having sex and feel worse and worse about myself and about our marriage. As friends were saying things like "I can't get my husband off of me! I can't even change in front of him because he always wants it," guilt and insecurities filled my mind. After months of frustration, I sat down with my husband and explained that I felt like we weren't having enough sex. He responded with "I never would have thought that. Why don't you ever tell me you want it or initiate?" I realized that I had carried the expectation that men will always pursue, and I hadn't shared my desire and drive with my husband. My sex drive is still higher than his, but instead of filling myself with guilt, I have now learned to talk with my spouse and show him my needs. Initiating isn't just a man's job! This has not only helped my internal struggle, but our marriage as well.

Problems or conflicts become much more manageable when you can talk them through without blaming or hurting one another. Spend time asking God to show you the right time, to give you a sensitive heart, and the right words to express yourself.

### *What if my husband never wants sex?*

We need to distinguish between a wife who has a higher sex drive and a marriage in which the husband never wants sex. One situation represents a normal difference in desire while the other likely indicates a deeper underlying problem.

If you tend to be the one to initiate sex, but your husband is eager and responsive, I wouldn't worry about it. While men *typically* think about sex more often than their wives, this is not always the case. There are some men who are more comfortable expressing love verbally or by enjoying activities with their wives. Other men avoid initiating sexually because they are afraid of rejection, but are eager to engage when their wife initiates.

While men and women have various sexual appetites, it's not normal for a man never to want sex with his wife. If your husband is simply not interested in sex, it's important for both of you to understand and address what is getting in the way of his desire for and enjoyment of sex. Sometimes, the problem is a physical roadblock, like thyroid disease, low testosterone levels, medications that interfere with sex drive or performance, obesity, or exhaustion. Stress, grief, and depression can also lower sex drive.

One question I'd encourage you to ask yourself: Do you think your husband feels dominated or overpowered by you? In some marriages in which a husband isn't sexually aggressive, he is also passive in other areas of the relationship. When a wife is bossy or critical, sometimes this impacts a man's confidence and results in sexual passivity. If this describes your marriage, I'd encourage you to pick up a book I wrote called *Finding the Hero in Your Husband* (Health Communications, Inc.) It will show you how to use your power as a wife to build up your husband in every area, including sexually.

Your husband could also be dealing with an emotional trauma like childhood sexual abuse. As difficult as it is for a woman to talk about molestation, it is infinitely more uncomfortable for men. Dr. Dan Allender's *The Wounded Heart* (NavPress) and Cecil Murphey's *When a Man You Love Was Abused* (Kregel Publications) are wonderful resources, in addition to counseling, in helping you and your husband work through painful past issues.

Sadly, some men have other sexual outlets that keep them from desiring sex with their wives. An extramarital affair, habitual masturbation, a sexual fetish he is too ashamed to admit, or porn use could all come between the two of you.

A lot of men were introduced to porn as boys and engaged with it throughout their teen and young adult life. The images from the past are seared into the brain and impact a man's sexual response in his marriage even years later. His brain is trained only to respond to more and more graphic sexual stimuli, so he is unable to enjoy normal sex with his wife.

As you might imagine, it is very difficult for a husband to admit to his wife that he is engaged with porn or some other form of immorality. Instead, he makes excuses and often continues secretly with porn, masturbation, or other sexual outlets that will keep up with the demand.

The encouraging news is that we *can* rewire our brains to learn a healthy sexual response. As porn impacts more and more marriages, God is raising up men and women to minister in this area of redeeming male and female sexuality. A list of trusted resources and counseling centers is included at 25questionsbook.com.

### *What about my needs?*

The truth is that while marriage is intended to fulfill our sexual needs and desires, millions of married men and women are sexually unsatisfied. Many who bail on marriage do so because of their sexual disappointment and frustration.

I encourage couples to do everything they can to meet each other's sexual needs. If sexual intercourse isn't possible, find other ways to enjoy sexual intimacy together. Teenagers seem to be able to figure out how to be sexually intimate without having sex—why can't we?

Don't allow this issue to be swept under the carpet. Even the Bible says that sex is an important part of marriage that should not be neglected. If your needs are vastly different than your husband's needs, work together to find the right balance or compromise for mutual sexual fulfillment.

You may have a spouse who is unwilling or unable to sexually satisfy you. While sex is an important part of marriage, remember that it is not the most important part. Marriages ultimately don't die because people stop having sex; they die when people stop keeping their promises.

God cares deeply about the covenant you and your husband made with each other. He also understands the limitations and longings of these bodies of ours. Because sex seems like such an earthy part of life, we often don't bring our sexual concerns and frustrations to God. I would encourage you, friend, to pour out your heart to the Lord. Ask Him to bless your sex life but also ask Him to use the difficulties and frustrations to help you become more like Him.

— How —

ADVENTUROUS

can we be in

BED?

# 8

After about ten years of marriage, I noticed that intimacy had become, well, boring. In fact, I was so bored with the "same old" sex that I calculated in my mind approximately how many times my husband and I had probably done the same thing. I figured that if we had sex on average twice a week, that was about a hundred times a year or a thousand times over ten years of marriage. Yeah, I know. Who thinks like that? The next thought I had was *Something's gotta change. My bedroom ceiling just isn't that fascinating!*

That little mental exercise was a wake-up call for me. I wanted sexual intimacy in my marriage to be fun, new, and creative. If sex was dull after ten years, how would I feel after thirty years of marriage?

I've wrestled with the question of how to make sex exciting while also showing reverence for God's standards. There are guidelines for things that are "out of bounds" for Christian couples (check out question 9), but you might be surprised at how much freedom we have to pursue adventurous sex in marriage. Consider the fact that the Song of Songs includes adventures like the bride planning a sexual rendezvous in a vineyard!

God created sex to be fulfilling to both men and women on many different levels. We have learned from scientific research that exciting, adventurous sex serves a different purpose in marriage than "normal" episodes of sexual intimacy. Both are important aspects of building a strong marriage.

### A chemistry lesson

To understand the importance of both "regular" and adventurous sex, it helps to know the impact each have on your body and brain. Although I loved school, I hated chemistry. So I'm going to make this as simple and painless as possible.

There are a lot of brain chemicals involved in sex. What you look at and what you think about has a powerful impact on what chemicals are flowing at any given time. When a couple in a committed relationship has sex, their bodies release endorphins and oxytocin. These two chemicals lead to feelings of closeness and bonding and also a general sense of well-being. Frequent "normal" intercourse in marriage literally helps a husband and wife feel closely connected as they weather the storms of life together.

When a couple has a new, exciting sexual experience, the body releases different chemicals, including phenylethylamine (PEA) and adrenaline. The combination of these two is powerful—much stronger than the steady impact of oxytocin and endorphins. In fact, PEA and adrenaline impact the brain in a way similar to crack cocaine. A person becomes intoxicated with sexual pleasure. God designed this as a wonderful treasure for young lovers to experience on their honeymoon as they venture into sexuality together and for lovers who find delight in exploring new things.

### *Two potential dangers*

Some couples err on the side of never trying anything new, sort of like I was ten years into marriage. Sex may become as routine as brushing your teeth or driving to work—just part of regular life.

I believe God gave us the incredible experience of renewed sexual pleasure so that married couples can enjoy "choice fruits, both new and old which I have saved up for you, my beloved" (Song of Solomon 7:13 NASB). In Proverbs 5:19, a young man is told to "ever be intoxicated" with sexual love for his wife. For this to be true, a couple needs to work on having fun, trying new things and yes, being adventurous.

On the other side of the spectrum is the couple that *always* seeks new and adventurous sex. There seems to be pressure to constantly push the envelope and achieve a new euphoric sexual high. This isn't healthy either. The chemicals that cause great sexual excitement are subject to the impact of tolerance.

In other words, what was exciting and arousing last week

won't be enough to achieve that same high today. Regular or "normal" sex just isn't good enough. This attitude leads to a couple desperate to find the next high and opens them up to sexual practices that are harmful and outside of God's plan, like bondage, dominance, sadism, and masochism (BDSM) or pornography. The search for a constant sexual "high" will eventually replace the emotional and spiritual intimacy that sex was meant to express. Loving each other gets lost in the quest for physical euphoria.

### *What's for dinner?*

How do you find the balance between staring at your bedroom ceiling and feeding a sexual addiction? The best illustration I've ever heard is comparing sex to cooking. (I'm not sure where I first heard it, so I don't know who to give credit to!) In your sexual relationship, there will be "fast food," "home-cooked meals," and "holiday feasts."

Fast food sex is all about meeting an immediate need. When you are exhausted and your husband desperately wants to be intimate, sometimes you just have sex to satisfy his immediate need (or vice versa). It may not be super-pleasurable or fulfilling for you, but it serves a purpose. This is much like stopping for fast food on a busy day. It fills your stomach temporarily, but you certainly don't want to make a habit of it.

Home-cooked sex is the basic standby. Usually it requires some thinking and planning ahead. You and your husband take time to enjoy each other physically, but there is no twelve-piece orchestra playing or fireworks display. You both are fulfilled sexually and emotionally—the interaction helps you feel connected and intimate.

A holiday feast happens every so often. The table is filled with rich and new foods to try. As on Thanksgiving or Christmas, you splurge in your celebration. This type of sex is important, even if it isn't frequent. It's for that weekend getaway or anniversary celebration. You and your husband put thought, planning, and set aside large quantities of time simply to explore and enjoy each other.

Trying new things in the bedroom isn't simply a matter of being adventurous. Sometimes it requires stepping outside of your comfort zone. The adventure might just as likely lead to laughter as it is to sexual pleasure. There may be times you might feel quite ridiculous trying something new. However, the desire to grow as a lover and to continue to enjoy the beautiful gift of intimacy is motivation for me to take Dr. Lewis Smedes's advice:

The Christian word on trying out a sexual practice that is not prohibited in Scripture is, "Try it. If you like it, it is morally good for you. And it may well be that in providing new delight to each other, you will be adventuring into deeper experiences of love."[2]

### *What's holding you back?*

One of the most common complaints I hear from Christian women is that they can't seem to enjoy sex. If you've read much about my own marriage journey, you know that I can relate. For many women, sexual pleasure just doesn't come naturally. Instead, we are aroused when we intentionally pursue our own sexual desire. This might start by giving yourself permission to enjoy sex and the freedom to discover what is physically pleasurable to you. Sex can't be only about pleasing your husband. God created you to experience pleasure as well.

While there are many unhealthy and immoral ways to wake up your sex drive, God's design is for a married woman to become aroused by meditating, even fantasizing, about her own husband. This may take effort, but it's worthwhile.

During the "boring seasons" of my marriage, I've sensed God asking me to make sexual pleasure a priority. I'm a goal-oriented person, but it took many years for me to realize that it is a godly goal to learn to be a great lover in marriage. A fulfilling sex life throughout the decades of marriage doesn't just happen. It requires commitment, time, and being intentional.

(Author's note: I highly recommend the ten-week Bible study Linda Dillow and I have created, *Passion Pursuit: What Kind of Love Are You Making?* [Moody Publishers]. It will help you dig deeper into God's Word—the why and the how to enjoy sex within marriage.)[3]

Is _____ OKAY in the BEDROOM?

(you fill in the blank!)

# 9

Because I speak and write books on sex, I get asked questions—a LOT of questions. The most common questions relate to "what's okay in the bedroom?" Questions like:

- Is oral sex okay? What about anal sex?
- Is it wrong to role-play with my husband?
- My husband likes to spank me. Is that okay?
- Do you think sex toys are wrong?
- What's wrong with a married couple watching porn together?

Before we even get into discussing whether something is right or wrong in the bedroom, I want to emphasize that God's desire is for you and your husband to experience GREAT PLEASURE!! His standards are not to limit your enjoyment, but to heighten it. I think many Christian couples have no idea what freedom they have in the bedroom. They settle for vanilla sex (aka the missionary position), placing self-imposed restrictions that have nothing to do with God's perspective. God made the marriage relationship a safe place for a husband and wife to explore, experiment, laugh, and get lost in sensational sex. Once you understand what God has said "no" to, you are free to have a great time exploring all He has given you to enjoy.

As with all areas of life, God's instructions on sex can be found in the Bible. The Bible talks about sex a lot, but often the answers to sexual questions aren't found in a chapter or verse. You won't find any references to vibrators, but using the Bible as a reference guide for decisions will make you wise in discerning good from evil (Hebrews 5:14) even when something seems like a grey area. There are three questions that can help you discern whether a sexual act is right or wrong in your marriage.

### Ask: Does God clearly say "no"?

If you are relatively familiar with the Bible, you might wonder about the difference between God's law expressed in the Old Testament and the New Testament teaching that Christians today are supposed to follow. There are a lot of rules in the Old Testament that we no longer adhere to. For example, we eat shrimp and wear clothes that have two different fabrics; both of these were forbidden for the Israelites before Jesus came.

The New Testament teaches that since Jesus came, we are now under a "new covenant." The strict rules that required sacrifice and physical purity were met through the perfect life, death, and resurrection of Jesus. However, we are still called to live moral lives that are "worthy of the Lord and please him in every way" (Colossians 1:10). Morality for Christians includes sexual purity (1 Thessalonians 4:3 and 1 Corinthians 6:18).

How do we define "sexual immorality"? By looking at the Scriptures passages that express God's design for sex and what God has said "no" to throughout the Old Testament and repeated in word or principle in the New Testament. These things probably won't surprise you but they also are not totally politically correct. Here's a list compiled by a friend and theologian, Dr. Jody Dillow:

1. ***Fornication:*** Fornication is immoral sex. This broad term includes sexual intercourse outside of marriage (1 Corinthians 7:2, 1 Thessalonians 4:3), sleeping with your stepmother (1 Corinthians 5:1), sex with a prostitute (1 Corinthians 6:15), and adultery (Matthew 5:32).

2. ***Adultery:*** Adultery, or sex with someone who is not your spouse, is a sin and was punishable in the Old Testament by death (Leviticus 20:10). In the New Testament, Jesus expanded adultery to mean not just physical acts, but emotional acts in the mind and heart (Matthew 5:28).

3. ***Homosexuality:*** The Bible is very clear that for a man to have sex with a man or a woman to have sex with a woman is wrong in God's eyes (Leviticus 18:22, 20:13, Romans 1:27, 1 Corinthians 6:9).

4. **Impurity:** There are several Greek words that are translated as "impurity." To become "impure" (Greek, *molyno*) can mean to lose one's virginity or to become defiled, due to living out a secular and essentially pagan lifestyle (2 Corinthians 7:1, 1 Corinthians 6:9). The Greek word *rupos* often refers to moral uncleanness in general (Revelation 22:11).

5. **Orgies:** For a married couple to become involved in sex orgies with different couples is an obvious violation of (1), (2), and (4).

6. **Prostitution:** Prostitution, which is paying for sex, is morally wrong and condemned throughout Scripture. (Leviticus 19:29, Deuteronomy 23:17, Proverbs 7:4–27).

7. **Lustful passions:** First, let me tell you what this does NOT mean. Lustful passion *does not* refer to the powerful, God-given sexual desire for each other enjoyed by a married man and woman. Instead, it refers to an unrestrained, indiscriminate sexual desire for men or women other than the person's marriage partner (Mark 7:21–22, Ephesians 4:19).

8. **Sodomy:** In the Old Testament, sodomy refers to men lying with men. The English word means male homosexual intercourse or intercourse with animals. Unfortunately, some Christian teachers have erroneously equated sodomy with oral sex. This is not the way the term is used in the Bible. The sodomites in the Bible were male homosexuals, or temple prostitutes (both male and female).

9. **Obscenity and coarse jokes:** In Ephesians 4:29, Paul

says, "Do not let any unwholesome talk come out of your mouths." The Greek word is very descriptive and literally means *rotten* or *decaying*. We have all been around people who can see a sexual connotation in some innocent phrase and then begin to snicker or laugh. This is wrong. However, this does not rule out sexual humor in the privacy of marriage, but rather inappropriate sexual comments in a public setting.

10. ***Incest:*** Incest, or sex with family members or relatives, is specifically forbidden in Scripture (Leviticus 18:7–18, 20:11–21).[2]

### Ask: Is it only between you and your husband?

Well, this question seems like a pretty obvious one. God said "no" to having sex outside of marriage and having sex with someone you're not married to. So, why do we even ask this question? Because many people are confused by where to draw the line. Is it okay, for example, to fantasize about a threesome even if you never intend to act it out in person?

Reserving sex, sexual fantasies, and sexual expression only for your husband means more than just what you do physically, but what you look at and what (and who) you think about. This is not my opinion; this is what Jesus said:

"You have heard that it was said, 'Do not commit adultery.' But I tell you that anyone who looks at a woman lustfully has already committed adultery with her in his heart" (Matthew 5:27–28).

This includes fantasy, pornography, online relationships, and erotica. This seems like a pretty strict standard. Jesus goes on to advise us on how to deal with temptation:

"If your right eye causes you to sin, gouge it out and throw it away. It is better for you to lose one part of your body than for your whole body to be thrown into hell." (Matthew 5:29)

His message is clear—get rid of whatever causes you to sin in your heart! Throw out the mommy porn. If it is a portal for temptation, get rid of your iPhone, satellite TV, or your Facebook account. Cut off the relationship that is tempting you. If you really want to know what God says, take His warning seriously. Stop flirting with anything that causes you to think, lust, or fantasize about someone other than your spouse.

### Ask: Is it good for me/us?

This is where things get fuzzy. I don't see anywhere in the Bible where God clearly says "no" to things like sex toys, anal sex, masturbation, or oral sex. In fact, you'll find very different opinions from Christian leaders on all these topics. The Corinthian church had questions about grey areas too. Instead of telling them exactly what to do, Paul gave them guidelines of how to use good judgment when the Bible doesn't clearly state something as right or wrong. Everything is permissible for me—but not everything is beneficial. Everything is permissible for me—but I will not be mastered by anything (1 Corinthians 6:12).

A few chapters later, Paul seems to repeat himself: Everything is permissible—but not everything is beneficial. Everything is permissible—but not everything is constructive. Nobody should seek his own good, but the good of others (1 Corinthians 10:23–24).

Here's what you can take from these passages. There are many things in life that you are free to do and enjoy. When you are not sure whether something is okay, put it through Paul's filter:

- Is this beneficial? Is it good for me? For my husband? Is it good for our marriage?
- Does it master me? Can it be habit-forming or addictive?
- Is it constructive? Does it help me grow and mature? Does it build our marriage?
- Is it loving? Does this action show love toward my husband or is it selfish?

This means that for some couples, a certain sexual act will be fine and, for another couple, the same sexual act isn't right for them. A good example of this is oral sex. Some couples feel great freedom to include this in their lovemaking. For other couples, oral sex is a trigger for memories of sexual abuse or pornographic images.

This also means that some sexual acts are not addressed in the Bible as a "no," but they still may not be good for you. A good example of this is BDSM, which stands for Bondage Dominance Sadism and Masochism. Experimenting with BDSM has become in vogue, largely because of the popularity of *Fifty Shades of Grey.* BDSM involves restraining, flogging, humiliating, and dominating your sexual partner for the purpose of pleasure. This kind of sex play involves harmful and potentially abusive elements that clearly are not beneficial or loving even if it is consensual.

Another question that often gets asked is, "Is it okay for me and my husband to engage in anal sex?" Although the Bible doesn't explicitly forbid anal sex, I would suggest that it's a bad idea, even within marriage, based on medical opinions that warn against it. That area of the body is contaminated with bacteria and has very thin skin tissue that is prone to tearing. As one doctor put it, "God made that an exit, not an entrance."

Do you wish God had given you a list of sexual acts with a clear "yes" or "no" by each one? It sure would make things a lot easier. But God, in His wisdom, has left some things open for a husband and wife to talk and pray through. You have to seek His wisdom for your own marriage. If you and your husband disagree on a "grey area," you will have to listen and learn to love each other through the decision.

After all, sex is a lot more than just sharing your body—it's a journey of intimacy. Figuring out the boundaries together gives you a great opportunity to seek the Lord's wisdom and to learn how to love each other more deeply.

WHAT *do my*
TEMPTATIONS
*say about*
ME?

# 10

I am tempted every day. Sometimes I'm disgusted by the thoughts that go through my head.

Daily life involves a continual battle of "kicking out" thoughts and impulses that I know aren't pleasing to God. I worry. I envy. I lust. Sometimes this feels as routine as other daily activities like brushing my teeth or eating. Other days, I'm hardly aware of temptation until it's too late—I've taken the bait.

Paul told the Roman church that the Christian life would be like this. There is a constant battle between the fleshly part of us that wants our own way and the spiritual part of us that longs to please God (Romans 6–7). We need God's grace and power every day for this battle.

Fighting temptation is hard enough, but it becomes exponentially more difficult when we heap guilt and shame on ourselves just because we are tempted. Many women feel defeated just by the fact that they are constantly tempted. This is particularly true with sexual temptations. "How could I be attracted to another man? I'm a married woman!" "Why do I keep having sexual dreams?" "Why can't I stop looking at porn?" If these statements describe you, let me assure you that you are not alone. Although every Christian is familiar with temptation, we often have misconceptions that set us up for defeat.

### *It is not a sin to be tempted.*

How do I know this? Hebrews 4:15 tells us that Jesus was tempted in every way but was without sin. You can be tempted by the same thoughts one hundred times a day without sinning. Satan loves to heap condemnation on us just for being tempted.

James 1:14–15 helps us understand how temptation transforms into sin and how we keep it from becoming sin. "Each person is tempted when they are dragged away by their own evil desire and enticed. Then, after desire has conceived, it gives birth to sin; and sin, when it is full-grown, gives birth to death."

Temptation becomes sin when we dwell on it and act on it. As my mentor, Linda Dillow, often reminds me, "You can't control what thoughts come into your mind, but you can control what stays there."

This is very important to understand. Godly men and women are tempted by all kinds of sin—porn, homosexual acts, cheating, pride, lying. What makes them godly is their desire to fight those temptations, on a daily basis if necessary.

We need to apply this principle not only to our own lives, but also to the lives of others. The other day, a woman asked me about her boyfriend's struggle with pornography. "We have started talking about marriage, so he wanted to let me know that porn has been an issue in his life. He has an accountability partner but says that it is still a daily battle for him. I don't know if I should consider marrying him if he has a problem with porn."

We all have the tendency toward sin. If we are honest, we would admit that we are tempted every day to have what we want on our terms. Instead of ignoring sin or pretending to have it all together, godly men and women are determined to be accountable to others and fight temptation.

### *Your temptations don't define you.*

With certain temptations seem to come labels.

"I'm a recovering alcoholic."
"She struggles with porn."
"He's a gossip."

I understand why we describe ourselves and other people this way, but I believe it's destructive. What you are tempted by should never define you.

How would you feel to learn that your pastor is tempted by lust? How about greed? Would it change your view of him just to know that he has been tempted? It shouldn't. If anything, our temptations tell us about the character of the enemy who wants to lie, steal, and destroy.

Paul wrote this to the Corinthian church:

Do not be deceived: neither the sexually immoral, nor idolaters, nor adulterers, nor men who practice homosexuality, nor thieves, nor the greedy, nor drunkards, nor revilers, nor swindlers will inherit the kingdom of God. And such *were* some of you. But you were washed, you were sanctified, you were justified in the name of the Lord Jesus Christ and by the Spirit of our God (1 Corinthians 6:9–11 ESV, emphasis added).

While sin once defined us, our current temptations don't. We are washed, sanctified, and justified. If you have trusted Christ for salvation, never accept a label, even in your own thinking, that defines you by your temptations or failings. By God's grace, old things have passed away and all things have become new.

### *The desire behind your temptation isn't wrong.*

The essence of every temptation is to offer a "shortcut" to meeting legitimate needs we experience. We want to feel significant, so we gossip about a friend. We want to be at peace, so we choose alcohol for a quick fix. We desire excitement, so we stir up interpersonal drama.

It's critical to distinguish between legitimate longings and unhealthy ways of meeting those needs. We do ourselves a great disservice when we condemn the healthy desires behind temptation. I've often seen this play out with sexual temptation. The desire for physical, emotional, and spiritual intimacy is God-given. You may be tempted to act out these desires in sinful ways, but there is nothing wrong with your longing. Instead of denying it, why not admit to the Lord that you are lonely and aching for intimacy?

When we are honest about our longings and desires, we will search for healthy, godly ways of meeting them.

God promises us that with every temptation also comes a "way of escape." When we call on Him, He will provide a way to address that anxiety, longing, or emotion that does not lead to sin.

Temptation isn't going away. We have an enemy who, like a roaring lion, prowls around looking to devour our faith. Yet, the Holy Spirit isn't going away either. He lives within you, giving you the wisdom and courage to stand.

How do I get
PAST
— my —
SHAME?

# 11

"What happens in Vegas stays in Vegas." You've heard the slogan, tempting us to believe that there is some place on earth where we can make mistakes but avoid the consequences. But sin just doesn't work that way. Whether you drive across the country, fly to Timbuktu, turn off all the lights, or push away the memories, the impact of past sin has a way of finding us. There is no arena of life where this is truer than with sexual sin.

*"You should be ashamed of yourself!"* It's a phrase you may have heard growing up when you hit your younger sister or stole a pack of gum from the grocery store. Yet no one had to tell you to be ashamed of yourself for other offenses, particularly related to sexuality. The problem is you can't *stop* feeling ashamed for what you've done or perhaps what has been done to you. Abortion, sleeping around, same sex experimentation, sexual abuse, pornography . . . they each can sentence women to a lifetime of shame. Even if you look put-together on the outside, the nagging

shame reminds you of your past—a past that always seems to define you.

I regularly meet women who are haunted by the shame of their sexual choices even decades later. Logically, they should have "moved on." Spiritually, they've heard that they are forgiven. Yet they can't shake the shame.

### What's the difference between guilt and shame?

Because we often use these two words interchangeably, it can be difficult to tease out the difference. Guilt is rooted in something we have done. We can be declared "guilty" by an authority like the legal system. Feelings of guilt are healthy when they reflect our true state of guilt, but we sometimes feel "false guilt" —guilty about things we have no responsibility for.

While guilt is rooted in what we have done, shame is the condemnation of who we are. Let me repeat that again. While guilt is rooted in what we have done, shame is the condemnation of who we are.

True guilt can lead to repentance and restoration, but shame looms like an oppressive cloud, separating us from knowing the love of Christ.

For many women, the world of sexuality represents a Gordian knot of shame and guilt that will be forever entwined. It seems impossible to separate actions and motives that we legitimately feel guilty about from the sense of being tarnished by violation and immoral sexual acts.

As a result of this confusion, there are many women who have trusted Christ but still live under a cloud of pervasive shame. They feel like "second-class" Christians, unable to experience the freedom for which Christ died. They have digested the lie that some sins are too dirty for Christ's blood to fully cleanse.

Here is what my friend Alice wrote about the shame from her past that plagued her marriage:

*My feelings of guilt and negativity were so powerful. They encompassed much of my private thought life and Satan had me nearly believing that I was one of the few Christian women who hadn't saved herself for marriage. This belief seemed to take on a life of its own. If I couldn't give my husband my purity, then everything else I did, no matter how much I loved him, was inadequate. I became so fixated on that lie that I began to wonder whether I could ever be the wife my husband deserved.*

Most women don't battle that kind of shame over a lie they told ten years ago or for gossiping about a friend. So why do sexual choices seem to create such lasting shame?

### *Are sexual sins unforgiveable?*

First Corinthians 6 seems to suggest that sexual sin is in a "different category" than other sin.

Don't you realize that your bodies are actually parts of Christ? Should a man take his body, which is part of Christ, and join it to a prostitute? Never! And don't you realize that if a man joins himself to a prostitute, he becomes one body with her? For the Scriptures say, "The two are united into one." But the person who is joined to the Lord is one spirit with him. Run from sexual sin! No other sin so clearly affects the body as this one does. For sexual immorality is a sin against your own body. Don't you realize that your body is the temple of the Holy Spirit, who lives in you and was given to you by God? You do not belong to yourself, for God bought you with a high price. So you must honor God with your body. (1 Corinthians 6:15–20 NLT)

Some of what Paul is teaching in this passage is hard to understand. He is describing a strong connection between our sexuality and our spirituality—that sexual choices have spiritual consequences. Recent research on sexuality and the brain supports the holistic impact of our sexuality. There is no such thing as "no strings attached" when it comes to sex. The images and memories of past sexual experiences can seem seared in your brain.

Because sexual sins are "different" than other sin, we often jump to the unspoken conclusion that they must be unforgivable. Alice expressed it this way:

*For years, Satan convinced me that sexual sin is somehow different from other sins—that choices like mine can't be redeemed. I struggled to accept that God's grace extended to my reality. After all, I hadn't been abused. I hadn't been forced to compromise my body. I chose it—and I chose it despite all of the good teaching of my parents and faith. I knew better.*

While sexual sins are dangerous and bring a host of potential consequences, they are not beyond God's forgiveness. In fact, the Gospels record Jesus forgiving sexual sins. Many of the women who came to Jesus were in bondage to sexual shame. He not only forgave them, He set them free.

### *How do you walk in the freedom of forgiveness?*

Like many other Christians, you may believe that Jesus forgives your sins enough to allow you into heaven, but you must bear the weight of them here on earth. The Father's love is great enough to save you from hell, but not to save you from shame. So you limp along, concluding that you have to settle for God's "plan B" for your life. When the guy you like doesn't call you, you conclude that this is God's way of giving you what you deserve. Or you relegate yourself to a passionless marriage. After all, why would God want you to experience great sex when you are so tainted?

I've got news for you—GOOD news. "It is for freedom that Christ has set us free" (Galatians 5:1). Freedom from shame, freedom from a "plan B" existence, and freedom from your self-condemnation. Like Alice, the truth of God's promises can set you free from the cloud of shame that has become your reality:

> *God challenged me to find in Scripture even one example of His limiting the gift of forgiveness. I looked and looked, but never found one. Instead, I re-discovered the blessing of boundless grace. God reminded me that His mercies are new every morning, and that reality forced me to believe that God hasn't segmented my sins. The journey to move past my shame has been long: six years into my marriage. I'm still walking the road toward freedom. I have seen the greatest progress during those times when I intentionally focus on who I am as a daughter of the Most High King. In His eyes, I am blameless, free, and forgiven. I am beautiful and worthy. His promises and His Word remind me of this truth. They also teach me that God can redeem my broken choices and transform my marriage into one which reflects His love.*

While Jesus paid a great price for your freedom, walking in it requires something from you:

If we claim to be without sin, we deceive ourselves and the truth is not in us. If we confess our sins, he is faithful and just and will forgive us our sins and purify us from all unrighteousness. If we claim we have not sinned, we make him out to be a liar and his word is not in us (1 John 1:8–10). Our sins are forgiven and cleansed when we acknowledge them. While you may walk in a constant stupor of shame, that doesn't mean that you have spoken to God about them. This is what king David experienced:

> When I refused to confess my sin, my body wasted away, and I groaned all day long. Day and night your hand of discipline was heavy on me. My strength evaporated like water in the summer heat. Finally, I confessed all my sins to you and stopped trying to hide my guilt. I said to myself, "I will confess my rebellion to the Lord." And you forgave me! All my guilt is gone. (Psalm 32:3–5 NLT)

Feeling guilty or shameful does nothing to bring freedom or to earn God's favor. God responds to an honest, broken, and contrite heart. Have you ever specifically confessed your sin to the Lord, asking for forgiveness? If not, put a stake in the ground right now. Get on your knees before the Lord and pour out your heart with confession. Ask for His forgiveness and thank Him for the precious gift of grace that frees us from hell, but also from shame.

While you cannot find a place on earth to hide from the consequences of sin, there is a reality in which your shame can be erased. Because what happened on the cross didn't stay on the cross, our Father God has promised that your sins will be remembered no more (Hebrews 8:12).

How do
I KNOW
HE is
the ONE?

# 12

*Is there one person I am meant to marry or should I just choose a good man?* This question isn't simply a contemplative exercise; it affects how you approach dating and marriage. However, I think it is the wrong question to be asking.

The question of "Is there one guy I'm supposed to marry?" is fundamentally based on fear. You've seen marriages break apart and wonderful romances turn ugly. Perhaps you grew up amid the turbulence of your mom and dad fighting. Judith Wallerstein, one of the foremost experts on the impact of divorce on adult children, noted that such survivors often cope with the reality of divorce by believing that true love is like winning the lottery. If you find your "soul mate," you can avoid the inevitability of broken vows and crushed dreams.

Christians have spiritualized this by placing their hopes of happily ever after on finding "THE ONE." When marriage gets difficult, a woman may panic, thinking, *Oh, no! I picked the wrong guy.*

Within the last year, I've met with two young Christian brides who walked away from their wedding vows before their third anniversary. Both of them based their decision to divorce on the thought that, "I never should have married him. I had doubts before the wedding and I didn't call it off." In essence, these young women believed since they married the wrong guy, their marriage covenant was "null and void" before God.

The truth is, whomever you marry, living out a lifetime commitment of love will be a challenge. One of the Bible's most romantic love stories is the account of Isaac and Rebekah, found in Genesis 24. If there were ever a situation in which God clearly said, "This is the one you should marry!" it was this couple. It was truly a match made in heaven.

Fast-forward a few decades. The star-crossed lovers are now parents of twin boys who despise each other. Isaac loves Esau and Rebekah loves Jacob. We find this husband and wife in a web of manipulation, anger, and deceit. Finding "the one" certainly didn't guarantee a lifelong, stress-free love affair. Selfishness and bitterness compromised their love even though they were ordained by God to fall in love and marry.

Instead of asking the question, "Is this the one I should marry?" consider these questions:

### Am I in God's will?

There are some things about your life that God has not clearly revealed to you. Perhaps you don't know who you should marry, what job you should take, or how many children you will have. Instead of spinning your wheels trying to figure out what you don't know, work to be the center of what God HAS revealed is His will for your life. As you seek love and marriage, God has given you some very clear guidelines of His will. Here is one of them: "It is God's will that you should be sanctified: that you should avoid sexual immorality" (1 Thessalonians 4:3).

Why would God reveal His specific will for you when you are not obeying His obvious will for you? For example, if you are sleeping with your boyfriend, you can know that this is NOT God's will for you. Have you stepped out of the place of obediently seeking Him and chosen to make decisions based on your own desires?

If you really want God to direct your steps toward the right man, be obedient to all you know He has asked of you. Read His Word, be faithful in prayer, keep your mind and your body pure, and give thanks for your current circumstances. God speaks to hearts that are prepared to listen and obey.

### *Am I seeking wisdom?*

Following God's leading isn't like looking for a message in the sky, telling you what to do next. Often, God leads through the wisdom of those he has put in our lives. Solomon repeats in Proverbs that the difference between a wise person and a fool is whether or not they are open to feedback (Proverbs 10:8).

There are general principles of wisdom that can help you in

dating and choosing a spouse. For example, it is wise to know a person for at least a year before making the commitment of marriage. You should meet his family and see him in many different types of circumstances. Take advantage of great books like Gary Thomas's book, *The Sacred Search.*

You should also be seeking very specific wisdom. In matters of dating and marriage, you will have some blind spots. There will be patterns and "red flags" around any relationship that are difficult for you to see. You may feel so "in love" and sure about a relationship that you can't imagine it turning sour. When a friend or parent raises a concern, do you write them off or even get angry? "You don't understand. You don't know him like I do!"

If you really want to know God's will, listen to those He has given you as friends and counselors. Ask for their feedback with questions like, "What do you see that I can't see? Are there any red flags you think I should be concerned about? Do you think we are moving too fast?" Don't just ask one person, ask a handful of advisors, some who are your age and others who have the wisdom of experience. And listen! Take to heart what they say. Be willing to break off a relationship or even an engagement if needed.

### Am I realistic about the covenant of marriage?

There are two extremes in the way young adults think and talk about marriage. While some are overly idealistic, most are fatalistic. For them, finding true love seems as improbable and random as being picked for a reality TV show. While you might fantasize about the possibility of finding the perfect man, you are more afraid of being fooled into a miserable marriage.

While every marriage has seasons of difficulty and disappointment, there are also times of great joy and celebration. Who you marry is a very important decision, but marital happiness isn't based on finding Prince Charming. The difference between intimacy and broken vows depends largely on the work you are willing to do within marriage. Any two people who are willing to grow and work through challenges can have a dynamic relationship.

In many ways, my husband and I were not well suited to be married to each other. Our backgrounds and personalities are extremely different. There were years when I wondered if I had married the right guy. We have very different philosophies on parenting, money, and work, but Mike and I have never considered divorce or a distant marriage as options. Even in seasons of disagreement, we've kept our love for each other and for the Lord intentionally front and center.

After over twenty years of marriage, I sincerely feel as if God handpicked my husband for me and me for him. I can't imagine being married to anyone else. I see the beauty of how our differences have challenged both of us to grow. Did God in His infinite power and wisdom pick Mike and me for each other? I don't know. What I do know is that He has taught us patience, gentleness, and humility—taking two very different people and making us one.

Expect that marriage will be a tremendous gift, but one that will require work and commitment. Expect that no matter who you marry, your concept of love will be refined. Expect that by leaning on the Lord, you will have everything you need to be a great wife. As 2 Peter 1:3 promises, "His divine power has given us everything we need for a godly life through our knowledge of him who called us by his own glory and goodness."

How FAR is TOO FAR ?

# 13

This age-old question is not only one teens are asking, but also women in their twenties, thirties, and beyond. With marriage often delayed and second marriages more common, women of all ages find themselves wondering about physical boundaries in dating.

If you are asking this question, first of all, good for you! More and more women no longer care about saving sex for marriage, even if they acknowledge it as God's best plan for them. Waiting seems to be too hard. Giving the sexual relationship a "test drive" sounds like a good idea (even though research solidly debunks this thinking). They fear losing the guy if they don't "put out." Or they may not even remember what they are supposed to be waiting for!

God's call to purity isn't just for teenagers. It's for men and women of all ages, married, divorced, and single. Yes, purity looks different at various stages of life, but the call to holiness doesn't change as you age. So what does it look like to date at 25, 38, 42, or 60? How far is too far?

The reason women ask this question is because the answer can be very complicated. If you are looking for a simple answer, I would say: "If you were wearing a fairly modest bikini, don't touch anywhere the bathing suit would cover." Yet that answer is unsatisfactory because it doesn't take into account variables like age, how long you've been dating, what causes your sexual engines to rev, or how pure your mind is even if you aren't touching.

### *A framework to think about*

A helpful way to think of sexual intimacy is to put it on a spectrum with other forms of intimacy. Every dating relationship has varying degrees of physical, emotional, and spiritual closeness. In healthy relationships, the degree of intimacy in every area progresses based on the level of commitment. In other words, sexual expression isn't going any further than trust, shared histories, seeking God together, and other aspects of intimacy. As a relationship slowly progresses, the couple becomes steadily more intimate in all areas.

The ultimate boundary of all intimacy is the marriage covenant. Marriage means making a lifelong promise of faithfulness. The wedding vows are meant to ensure that you will not be rejected or discarded by the one you share your body, your heart, and your soul with. Only marriage provides the "all systems go" assurance of safety and fidelity.

The problems I most commonly see in dating are these:

**(1) Physical intimacy quickly races forward, ignoring other aspects of intimacy.**

A couple begins making out, intimate touching, and so on without any history, commitment, or connection. The ecstasy of physical touch becomes the center of their relationship. Regardless of whether they have crossed some subjective line of "going too far" sexually, they've given away and taken more than they should have. Their relationship really isn't based on mutual respect, but on mutual self-gratification. Even if they haven't had sex, the woman probably feels used, dirty, and defiled. Maybe you can identify with this. Have you ever felt "cheap" or "violated" just by kissing someone you hardly knew?

Women sometimes ask what they can do while dating and still be a virgin. Can she still technically wear a white dress if she's experienced everything except for intercourse? The issue isn't about virginity—it's all about pursuing purity. A better question to ask is, "Am I honoring God with my body?" If the answer is no, ask God to show you how to honor Him from this day forward.

**(2) Christian couples are hypersensitive to physical boundaries but pay no attention to emotional or spiritual boundaries.**

Have you ever known a couple that has been dating for three months but act like they are married? They cut off other friendships and exclusively spend time together. They have pet names for each other and celebrate an anniversary each month. They share their deepest secrets and temptations, including sexual failures. They plan their futures together, promising never to break up.

Please understand this: These boundary violations are just as dangerous as being sexually intimate! In many cases, sharing deeply on the spiritual and emotional level makes staying sexually pure almost impossible. Just as a couple needs to "pace themselves" sexually, they also need to be careful about how quickly they progress in emotional and spiritual intimacy.

You may never have considered that you can be too spiritually or emotionally intimate in a dating relationship. In the sexual arena, you can see how far you've progressed. It's a little more complicated to assess intimacy emotionally and spiritually—plus, no one talks about it being a danger. For example, I'm not sure it is appropriate early in a relationship for a man and woman to pray or study the Bible together alone. One older woman who had her heart broken in a relationship made the commitment that she would never make a meal for a man she wasn't married to. Why? Because to her it symbolized the intimacy and nurture of a marriage commitment. These are very personal decisions based on the truth that giving away too much of your heart can be as painful as giving away too much of your body. Have you ever thought through "how far is too far" in these areas?

### A game plan

I'll admit that I'm the planner type. For better or for worse, I think through everything. When my husband, Mike, and I were dating, I was hypersensitive to boundaries because I was afraid of making a mistake. I didn't want my hormones to hijack my reasoning. One day, Mike playfully kissed me all over my face. Instead of delighting in this romantic gesture, I stopped him by saying, "What do those kisses mean? They don't mean anything!" Yes, it's a miracle that the guy ended up marrying me!

Fortunately for my teenage boys, I've mellowed just a bit. I understand the fun of dating and the thrill of romance. However, I also recognize how powerful passions and drives can lead to disaster if not managed. You don't have to be as unromantic as I was, but you do need to be proactive about setting your boundaries. Here's what I suggest.

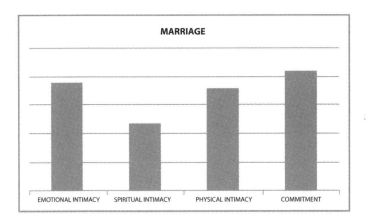

Using a graph like this one, chart your relationship on levels of intimacy. Let your level of commitment be the bar that sets the pace for each aspect of intimacy. Where do you think it is appropriate to be at this stage of your relationship? What area of intimacy seems to be speeding ahead of the others? Realistically, how long would it be before there is the potential of marriage? Are you setting yourself up for trouble by the "pacing" of intimacy in your relationship?

Proverbs reminds us that without many "advisers," plans fail—but with this counsel, they succeed (15:22 ESV). No one is beyond this principle. You are never too old, too experienced, or too wise to need godly counsel, especially in the area of romantic relationships. Be sure you have a few friends and mentors who will ask you hard questions, give advice, and pray with you as you make decisions about boundaries in all areas of your relationship.

Is LIVING TOGETHER a good TEST RUN for MARRIAGE?

14

Getting married is one of the biggest decisions you will ever make. If marriage is a lifetime commitment, then why not have a "trial run" before making it official?

Over 50 percent of couples do exactly this. Living together before marriage is becoming increasingly prevalent, even among Christian couples. They reason that trying it out before marriage just makes sense. This is particularly a strong argument for those who are hesitant about a lifetime commitment. Having witnessed or experienced the pain of divorce, they know that a beautiful wedding in a packed church doesn't guarantee happily ever after.

I want to share with you a few reasons why cohabitation is a bad idea. If your goal is to someday have a loving, stable relationship, living together before marriage is far more likely to sabotage lifelong intimacy than be a stepping-stone for it.

### *What does the research say?*

In spite of the "wisdom of the day" that cohabitation is a wise test drive, the research indicates that living together before marriage may actually increase your risk for divorce in the future. Many experts believe that the "squishy" approach toward commitment represented by cohabitation sets a couple up for bailing on marriage when things get difficult. Holding sexual fidelity and the marriage covenant as sacred before God impacts your willingness to work through the challenges of life together.

Dr. Scott Stanley, psychologist and research professor at the University of Denver, calls this *sliding* instead of *deciding*:

> The core idea is that people often slide through important transitions in relationships, such as starting to live together, rather than deciding what they are doing and what it means . . . we have found that fully two-thirds of the sample of cohabiters report a process more like sliding into cohabitation than talking about it and making a decision about it. There used to be many steps and stages of courtship and relationship development that, for the most part, no longer exist. Does that mean it's harder than ever to make clear commitments? I suspect so. In contrast to sliding, commitments that we are most likely to follow through on are based in decisions. In fact, one essential truth of commitment is that it means making a choice to give up other choices. A commitment is a decision.[1]

Research also tells us that couples living together are more likely to experience sexual unfaithfulness, domestic violence, and higher levels of relational unhappiness. Bottom line—if you are living with your boyfriend with the hope to avoid heartbreak, you are likely setting yourself up for failure.[2]

### *Cohabitation is intimacy on a man's terms.*

Glenn Stanton, author of *The Ring Makes All the Difference,* believes strongly that the growing trend toward cohabitation is putting women at risk. While women have great power in the marriage relationship, they have relatively little leverage as a live-in. Stanton argues that cohabitation puts men in the driver's seat. They get what they want (sex and companionship) without giving what they fear (commitment).[3]

Stanton's survey of the research on cohabitation led him to this conclusion: "Women are more likely to see their cohabiting relationships as a conveyer belt to marriage. Guys are more likely to see their cohabiting relationships as an opportunity to see each other more often, have fun together, make sure he's taken care of, and gain access to more regular sex."[4] In fact, men who end up getting married display less commitment to their spouses even after they get married.[5]

While this may be painting with a broad brush, I think Glenn is hitting on a fundamental truth. To a large degree, men are convinced to commit to marriage because they long for companionship and a sexual partner. When a guy has a "live-in" sexual companion and partner, he has little reason to make a commitment. When a woman makes marriage the condition for giving herself to a man, she may lose a guy who has no interest in commitment, but she will challenge a "good man" to take the step of marriage covenant. The gold standard of saving yourself for a lifetime commitment asks men to become men and flushes out the guys who aren't willing to display the unselfishness required in a long-term relationship. Don't settle for anything less!

### *Cohabitation is taking yourself out of God's will.*

There is nothing I fear more than being out of God's will. I've seen enough pain and devastation in this world to know that I need God. I need His wisdom and comfort every hour of every day. As Mike and I navigate the challenges of raising three boys and living life together, we know that on our own, it's not enough. No amount of psychological training, self-help books, or willpower can adequately equip me for life on planet Earth.

I find tremendous comfort knowing that I can cry out to God and trust Him to give me wisdom no matter what comes our way. Even when I don't "feel" His presence, I know He is there. Why? Because He has promised me that He will draw near to me when I draw near to Him. Access to God's wisdom and comfort is largely dependent upon our willingness to "abide" in Him—to walk in obedience. First John 1:6–7 says, "If we claim to have fellowship with him and yet walk in the darkness, we lie and do not live out the truth. But if we walk in the light, as he is in the light, we have fellowship with one another, and the blood of Jesus, his Son, purifies us from all sin."

By choosing to ignore God's teaching on marriage and sexuality, you are electing to walk in darkness and to do life on your own terms. You can't claim the rich promises of God while living in stubborn rebellion against His expressed will for you. Frankly, by living with your boyfriend, you are rejecting the fellowship of God. Romance, marriage, sex, family—these are complicated aspects of life. Don't reject the Counselor who can give you the wisdom and strength to navigate them well.

### *Now what?*

Maybe you are convinced that a "test run" is a bad idea, but you are reading this book snuggled up against your live-in boyfriend. Now what? How do you go backwards in your relationship? If you insist on marriage, you may lose your best friend.

I'm not just talking to the twenty-five-year-old college grad. The message is the same for the fifty-five-year-old who doesn't want to give up the financial benefits of alimony or life insurance by getting married. Sexual purity isn't just for young adults. All who claim to be disciples of Jesus are told to be set apart as holy.

The good news is that God is a Master at working out messes when we bring them to Him. Jesus would say to you as He said to so many women in messes. "I don't condemn you. Now leave your life of sin."

Taking a stand to be sexually pure when you've already crossed that line takes a step of faith. It means that you may have to temporarily create an earthquake in your life. The ground that seemed steady will shift, but consider for a moment the ground that for now seems so steady. Do you want to live your life with a man who threatens to leave if you stand on your integrity?

Jesus told a story of two homes—one built on the sand and the other on the rock. Both houses looked great when the weather was calm. But when the storms came, the house on the sand crumbled while the one built on the rock stood. Please consider that you are building a house. The decorations and the style are negotiable, but the foundation you choose is absolutely critical. My friend, "playing married" without the sacred commitment of marriage is choosing to build on an unstable and volatile foundation. I urge you to bring your "mess" before Jesus and ask Him to show you how to rebuild on the truth of His unchanging Word!

What if I'm ATTRACTED — to — SOMEONE ELSE?

# 15

The stereotype of an adulterous affair in marriage has typically been the picture of a cheating husband. The man has a one-night stand on a business trip or falls in love with his coworker. I guess it never occurred to us that for every cheating man, there must also be a cheating woman.

Relationship expert Bonnie Eaker Weil reported on ABC's *20/20* her findings that over 50 percent of married women are sexually unfaithful.[1] That statistic doesn't take into consideration the countless others who are entangled in emotional affairs and fantasies.

Every married woman is at risk for an affair. If you say, "No, I'd never do that!" take to heart what Paul wrote, "If you think you are standing firm, be careful that you don't fall!" (1 Corinthians 10:12).

An affair always begins with a temptation—an attraction. Unfortunately, most of us have no idea what to do when a man other than our husband starts to pay attention to us. It feels good to be pursued again, especially if your marriage has become tedious.

Right after Paul told us to be careful not to fall, he gave some very practical advice about how to handle temptation:

> No temptation has overtaken you except what is common to mankind. And God is faithful; he will not let you be tempted beyond what you can bear. But when you are tempted, he will also provide a way out so that you can endure it. (1 Corinthians 10:13)

While temptation is unavoidable, sin is still inexcusable. Even if you feel overwhelmingly attracted to another man (or woman), unfaithfulness doesn't have to be your destiny. God has promised to provide a way out for those who are willing to run to Him.

### *Don't be surprised when it happens*

How many affairs would be avoided if we would simply anticipate that it's normal to be tempted? Yes, there will always be men more attractive than your husband, and there will be someone who seems to have all the strengths that your husband lacks. The day will likely come when you find yourself drawn to someone who appears to be better suited for you than your husband. The attraction can even be spiritual—this man's passion for the Lord is so attractive compared to your husband who seems to be spiritually dead.

Since you know this day will come, prepare for it now. Remember in elementary school all the times you had a fire drill or tornado drill? Why do we have fire drills? To prepare for a real danger during a time that is not a crisis. Using that same wisdom, come up with a plan now of what you will do when temptation comes. How will you respond? Who will you call for help?

Do you have an accountability partner in place now? What woman in your life have you told, "You have permission to ask me the hard questions about my marriage. I want you to get in my face if you ever see something in my life that concerns you."

Just like the fire drill, if you have already determined where to "run," you won't be paralyzed when a true danger threatens your marriage.

### Remember what's real

I had been meeting with Lisa for about two months before she spilled the beans. During our first several counseling sessions, she talked around her disappointment in marriage and other irritations of life. Then, the day came when she felt safe enough to tell me about Doug. They had met at the gym several months earlier and been drawn to each other immediately. Lisa and Doug began "coincidentally" showing up at the gym at the same time and got to know each other. Eventually, they began meeting over coffee.

"Juli, Doug is so kind and sensitive! He loves God and has

really helped me grow in my faith. God knows how lonely I've been in my marriage. I believe He's providing Doug as an answer to my prayer for true companionship."

Okay . . . reality check. God will NEVER answer your prayers by inviting you into sin. How could a grounded Christian woman like Lisa have gotten so far off base? Because Satan is the deceiver. He will tempt you to doubt the truth about what is good and what is evil.

God has equipped our bodies with very powerful hormones that kick in when we enter a new romantic relationship. Remember when you could go days without thinking about food or when you wrote your boyfriend's name all over your geometry notebook? Your mind still has the capacity to experience "puppy love," even as a grown woman.

The anticipation of a new relationship can feel exciting and will blind you from reality. If you do not fight to find "true north" according to God's Word, you will make a disastrous decision that has far-reaching consequences. No matter how much you believe that this man will make your life better, he will NOT. No amount of money, great sex, or adoration can compensate for walking away from communion with God and representing Jesus Christ to your husband, children, and community.

### Run fast

There is a time to walk and then there is a time to run. No one casually strolls out of a burning building. They run for their lives. Paul says sexual temptation represents a time to run. "Flee sexual temptation!" Joseph demonstrated what "fleeing" looks like. He literally ran away from Potiphar's wife when she tried to seduce him. He didn't stop to deliberate the consequences or figure out how he could keep the woman happy while not going "all the way." He simply ran (Genesis 39:6–12).

*There's no harm in a little flirting*, you might think. Yes, there is great harm. The longer you linger in temptation, the more opportunity the enemy has to deceive you.

What does "running" look like? It means not giving the relationship any chance to develop. If you have to, change jobs, move to another neighborhood, and absolutely refuse to be alone with the person who represents the temptation.

### *Ask for help*

One of the most dangerous things to do when you are attracted to another man is to keep it your little secret. You may be embarrassed to admit to a friend your secret crush, or you may be afraid that being honest will mean you have to give it up.

In some cases, I think it's appropriate to tell your husband. "Honey, I just need you to know that there is a guy at work who I've committed to never being alone with. Nothing has happened, but I just sense it's a danger zone." It would be very difficult for an attraction to take root after this type of honest conversation.

If you do not believe it is wise to talk to your husband, please share the situation with a trusted friend or mentor. She can pray with you, give you solid advice, and ask you the tough questions about whether or not you are taking the way of escape or continuing to play with fire.

### Invest in your marriage

If you've ever had a serious health concern, it probably changed the way you approached your health. A near-fatal heart attack will cause most of us to swear off fatty foods. The same should be true of how we respond to the possibility of a broken marriage. It should cause us to reexamine what we've begun to take for granted.

I know you've heard the statement, but it's worth repeating, "The grass is greener wherever you water it." Being attracted to another man is not only a temptation, but also an indication that perhaps your marriage needs some watering. It's a "wake-up" call that your marriage is vulnerable to infidelity. Can you pinpoint what desires you have that are not being met in your marriage?

Maybe it's time to invest in marriage counseling, get away for some time alone with your spouse, or work on romance and sexual satisfaction in your marriage. Even if you are married to an unresponsive husband who doesn't have a strong desire to improve your marriage, how are *you* investing in the relationship? Do you pray daily for God to give you love and patience? Are you intentional about learning how to build intimacy, as far as it depends upon you?

Although investing in your marriage is an important way to respond to a temptation, investing in your relationship with God is even more important. There are some who believe that the greatest weapon against an affair is a strong marriage. I disagree. The greatest weapon against a spiritual threat (and temptation is a always a spiritual threat) is a spiritual weapon.

Paul told us specifically how to arm ourselves against the schemes of the devil. He told us to be clothed with the armor of God—armor like the breastplate of righteousness, the belt of truth, the shield of faith, and the sword of the spirit (Ephesians 6:10–17).

My friend, never try to fight a spiritual temptation solely with emotional or psychological weapons. You will lose. God's way of escape is to cling to Him and to run to Him. He is able to keep you from stumbling, and to make you stand in the presence of His glory blameless with great joy (Jude 24).

If I remain faithful throughout the duration of my marriage, it won't simply be because I love my husband, but will be because of how much I love the Lord. Clinging to Mike might keep from wandering, but only clinging to Jesus can make my heart pure.

*The name of the Lord is a fortified tower;*
*the righteous run to it and are safe.* Proverbs 18:10

How can
I COMPETE
—with—
PORN?

# 16

A young wife recently told me, "Last night I walked in on my husband looking at porn. This isn't the first time this has happened. I feel so violated—like I could never share my body with him again. Why should I, anyway? I could never compete with porn!"

If your husband has been involved with pornography, you know the feeling of betrayal in discovery. You question everything: his love for you, your desirability, and his credibility. Every sexual experience you've ever had with your husband is now viewed through a different lens.

The issue of porn has become increasingly common among women as well. It's no longer "Every Man's Battle" but is now "Every Marriage's Battle." When meeting with a married couple, I no longer ask *if* it has played a role in the husband or wife's life. Instead, I ask *what role* it has played in their lives. Even a man or woman who isn't tempted by porn has seen it and been impacted by it.

In one respect, sexual intimacy between a husband and wife *can't* compete with pornography. Porn is selfish sex, requiring no sacrifice and no effort to love another person. You can have what you want, when you want, how you want it. Sex with a real person requires patience, communication, delaying what you want to meet the needs of the other person.

A man whose sex drive is hyped up on porn will have great difficulty enjoying the beauty of sex with his wife. Research consistently demonstrates that men who regularly watch porn rate their sexual partners as less attractive than men who don't view porn. Pornographic material fuels the allusion that fantasy and a sexual release will bring satisfaction. Instead of satisfying, it leads to an insatiable desire for more. If you are trying to *compete* with the pornographic images on a computer screen, you are out of luck. Ironically, porn can't even compete with itself. A man using porn doesn't go back to the same picture or video, but always wants something new, more exciting and provocative. However, we must remember that porn is NOT intimacy; it is a cheap counterfeit. Your husband needs more than sex; he was designed for intimacy.

Couples who experience true intimacy know how to fully share their sexuality—how to communicate the most intimate of experiences with and without words. Being emotionally naked makes you extremely vulnerable. Both you and your husband have to feel completely safe to let go, to share thoughts, desires, and physical sensations. The journey toward authentic intimacy is one of creating the safest environment possible so that you can explore together without fear of betrayal or humiliation. Porn does the exact opposite. It makes your bedroom an emotional landmine.

As rampant as pornography and sexual addictions have become, God is still in the business of healing. No one is beyond His redemption and restoration. As you seek authentic intimacy in your marriage, here are a few practical steps to take.

### *Have empathy for your husband's struggle*

Most women understandably react to the issue of porn with anger and disgust. Typically the use of pornography has been hidden, so a wife feels lied to and betrayed, adding to her feelings of righteous anger. If this describes you, you have reason to feel the way you do. Sexuality in marriage is a sacred trust, and that trust has been broken. However, lambasting your husband is not likely to result in restored intimacy.

Although it was written thousands of years ago, before the creation of *Playboy,* the Bible has some wise, relevant, and practical advice for how to deal with a husband's porn use. "First take the log out of your own eye, and then you will see clearly to take the speck out of your brother's eye" (Matthew 7:5 NASB, Luke 6:42).

You may be thinking, *I don't look at porn! I've done nothing like that to offend my husband.* Jesus is teaching the principle that we all are sinners. Being honest with our own sinful hearts prepares us to respond with kindness and forgiveness, even when we are confronting someone.

Although you may not understand your husband's sexual temptations, you know what it feels like to battle against sin. Empathy begins with humility, the acknowledgment that you are just as flawed and broken as your husband is. Your sin of choice could be self-righteousness, the desire to be esteemed by others, gossip, bitterness, complaining, dishonesty, or even wishing you had a different husband.

Jesus constantly reminds us of how much we have been forgiven so that we have a heart that is ready to extend mercy when others offend us.

Empathy also means understanding that good men are tempted by sexual sin. Christians who struggle with sexual temptation can carry an enormous amount of shame. Just the fact that they are *tempted* to look at porn or think sexually about a coworker brings about thoughts like:

*What's wrong with me? No matter how hard I try, I can't stop thinking this way!*

*I hate myself for the thoughts I have. If anyone knew what really went through my mind, they would be sickened.*

I have met wonderful Christian men who doubt their salvation because the fight against lust is so great. A godly husband is NOT a man who doesn't struggle with sexual sin, but one who continually fights and refuses to give in to temptation.

### *Call your husband to purity*

Empathy does NOT mean excusing sin. Our hearts should never be so "soft" that we look the other way instead of confronting. While some wives have a difficult time understanding why their husbands struggle sexually, others approach the issue as if it is not a big deal. This is particularly true with porn. I've heard wives buy into this thinking with statements like: "It's not like he's having an affair. Plus, it takes pressure off of me having to always satisfy him."

While Jesus extends overwhelming grace and forgiveness to us in our sin, He also calls us to pursue purity. As a godly wife, you are called to help your husband set his eyes on a standard of holiness in your marriage. But how do you do this?

One of the primary ways you can help your husband is to link his behavior with the impact on your marriage. Satan deceives men into compartmentalizing their sexual sin. In other words, a man may believe that he can fantasize about another woman, flirt with someone at work, or look at sexual pictures on the Internet and that this has no impact on how deeply he loves his wife.

Sexual sin of any kind destroys the possibility of intimacy between you and your husband. You can help him make this link by sharing your thoughts like this wife did in a letter to her husband:

*Dear Craig,*

*It's difficult for me to express to you how I feel about the pornography issue. I have not had the temptation to look at porn, so I admit that I don't really understand what a struggle it is for you. I want to understand how to help you and pray for you, but I also need you to know how pornography affects me. When we said, "I do" I gave myself to you, body, soul and spirit. I want to be your best friend and to build a great sex life together. But I feel violated knowing that you may be thinking of a naked stranger when you are with me. I can't let myself go with you—I don't feel safe.*

*Intimacy in our marriage is worth fighting for. I'm ready to do whatever it takes to make our marriage a safe place for both of us. But I need your promise and commitment to say "no" to every other woman (even those in a picture) in order to say "yes" to me.*

*I love you,*
*Sherry*

If your husband is open about his struggle, asking for forgiveness, and wanting help, do all that you can to support him. If however, he denies that it is a problem and refuses to address it, you need to draw boundaries and create an atmosphere that does not enable sin to continue. These decisions require great discernment, which is why Scripture tells us to bring in a wise third party (pastor or counselor) to help us walk biblically.

### *Fight like a team*

One of the most damaging aspects of sexual temptation is that it divides couples. Rarely will a husband and wife discuss how they are tempted sexually unless one of them catches the other in the act. Because of the shame and feelings of rejection associated with sexual temptations, most people keep it a secret from their spouse.

As much as Satan would love to have one or both of you fall into sexual sin, he is happy to use the temptation itself as a wedge between you. The last thing he wants is for you and your husband to work together in combating temptation.

Remember who the true enemy is. Regardless of which of you struggles with sexual temptation, you must begin to see this as your problem as a couple. I don't mean that a wife should take responsibility for her husband's purity or vice versa. However, when sexual sin and temptation hits one of you, it impacts both of you. Satan will use pornography, inappropriate emotional attachments, and other forms of temptation to further divide you if he can define your spouse as "the problem" or "the enemy." As long as you are fighting each other, you cannot stand together.

Mike and I have learned over the years what it means to fight temptation as a team. At first, it seemed like an invasion of privacy to ask each other about how we were tempted. Then we realized that it was actually a step toward deep intimacy to be so vulnerable with one another. Fighting together against the enemy has deepened our trust in one another and profoundly impacted our intimacy.

Being a team doesn't mean being each other's primary accountability partner. Although it is healthy for a husband and wife to understand how and when the other is most tempted, you need a woman you trust to ask you the difficult questions and he needs another man to do the same for him.

Mike and I have also learned that being a team means playing "offense" not just defense. In other words, we want to have an exciting sexual relationship and enjoy each other as friends. Sexual temptations are not as powerful when intimacy in marriage is satisfying.

Ecclesiastes 4:12 can easily be applied to marriage:

Though one may be overpowered, two can defend themselves. A cord of three strands is not quickly broken.

This verse speaks of a cord of three strands. Remember that the Christian marriage is not made up of two, but of three. You and your spouse do not stand against the enemy by yourselves. You stand with the person of the Lord Jesus Christ ready and able to fight with and for you. The Lord's opinion of your marriage is not neutral. He says in Hebrews 13:4 that the marriage bed should be pure and marriage should be honored by all. The Almighty One also declares that whom He has joined together, let no one tear apart. Begin fighting the true enemy of your marriage as a team by reminding one another that "if God is for us, who can be against us" (Romans 8:31)?

One final note: It is important to understand the difference between sexual temptation and a sexual addiction. Although the psychological community is still debating the symptoms of sexual addiction, we know that it typically involves compulsively thinking about sex, engaging in high-risk behavior (like looking at porn at work or paying for prostitution), and an inability to stop these behaviors despite repeated attempts. Please understand that a sexual addiction, like any addiction, isn't going to go away with normal marriage interventions. If you or your husband have symptoms of a sexual addiction, please reach out to someone who is trained psychologically and spiritually to address this issue. Here are a few ministries to follow up with: stonegateresources.org and purelifeministries.org.

What's WRONG
— with —
MOMMY
PORN?

# 17

Over the past several years, much of my job has involved engaging in the issue of mommy porn, thanks to *Fifty Shades of Grey*. Porn for women and erotica have always been around, but not until recently has it become acceptable for Christian women. I regularly receive emails from women who see no problem with reading erotic novels. They have often been told by Christian friends that "mommy porn" is a good way to spice up your sex life. When I meet with young women, I regularly hear stories of their porn addictions. What was once only considered a man's problem has now become an issue that women confront as well.

Pornography, including erotica, is created for the purpose of manufacturing sexual arousal. Yes, books like *Fifty Shades* may get your juices flowing, but please don't confuse sexual excitement with sexual intimacy. Ultimately, mommy porn sabotages intimacy in marriage and intimacy with God. Here's why.

### *Erotica leads to false intimacy*

Material like *Fifty Shades of Grey* fuels the illusion that fantasy and a sexual release will bring satisfaction. Instead, it leads to an insatiable desire for more. As I said earlier, men and women who engage in pornography and erotica will ultimately be *less* satisfied in their intimate relationships and may even find themselves leaving their marriage to chase the next elusive sexual high. This isn't theoretical—I've heard from several women who are living out this very scenario.

Research consistently demonstrates that pornographic material decreases your sexual pleasure in real relationships. Doff Zillman and Jennings Bryant studied the impact of repeated exposure to porn on intimate relationships. "After consumption of pornography, subjects reported less satisfaction with their intimate partners—specifically, with these partners' affection, physical appearance, sexual curiosity, and sexual performance proper. In addition, subjects assigned increased importance to sex without emotional involvement. These effects were uniform across gender and populations."[2]

These same findings translate to the impact of "mommy porn." I recently received this email from a woman who had this to say:

*Last year I stepped into this 50 shades trap. I couldn't stop reading. When I finished the first book, I borrowed money to buy the other two. In the evening I would tell my husband every detail of what I have read that day. My life literally revolved around 50 shades. I also expected my husband to "be" Christian Grey. Suddenly our sex life thrived! We tried new things, we went wild. And just as suddenly we hit rock bottom. We were constantly fighting; in my eyes my husband couldn't do anything right. We grew apart. I defended the book and said there's nothing wrong with it. But to be honest, it almost destroyed my marriage.*

Porn and erotica are sex on demand. You don't have to wait for the right guy—or any guy, for that matter. You can instantly experience sexual excitement and release. The problem is that it's all fake. You are not in a relationship with the naked person on the computer screen or the irresistible millionaire portrayed in an erotic novel. You are responding sexually to one-dimensional characters with whom you have no authentic connection.

The more you chase the counterfeit, the further away you get from the real deal—intimacy. Becoming a great lover requires you to exercise the muscles of temporarily suspending what you want in order to understand and bring pleasure to your partner. Mommy porn teaches you to chase after your immediate desire with no thought of love.

### *Erotica denies sexual realities*

One of the most widely known fantasy stories starts out like this: "A long time ago, in a galaxy far, far away . . ." From the outset, Star Wars asks you to step away from what you know to be true and imagine a different galaxy, a different time, with different assumptions —plus Wookies and talking robots, time warps, and space travel.

Erotica also lures you into a different reality, but it doesn't announce that you are entering a world "far, far away." Within the context of "normal life," erotica introduces romantic stories that are not possible. But just as our universe is governed by scientific laws such as gravity, there are also principles that govern our emotions, relationships, and spiritual health. You have freedom to choose if you will abide by them, but you can never be free from the consequences of your actions. If you eat chocolate cake and potato chips all day, every day, your body will not function as it should. If you jump out of a second-story window, you will (at best) break a few bones. Although the consequences are not as immediate or obvious, you cannot violate spiritual laws without also experiencing harm.

Erotica twists and distorts the results of making immoral and foolish choices. In the real world, our actions have consequences, sometimes very grave consequences. The authors of erotica simply ignore or erase those consequences and create a magical "happy ending." King Solomon wrote a proverb (6:27–28) thousands of years ago that echoes the danger of this type of fantasy: "Can a man (or woman) scoop fire into his lap without his clothes being burned? Can a man walk on coals without his feet being scorched?"

The popularity of *Fifty Shades* has deceived many into believing that there are no natural or spiritual consequences for sinful choices. The Bible clearly teaches that our sinful choices keep us from the greatest intimacy—intimacy with God.

Satan's agenda has always been to confuse us about right and wrong, and he has succeeded. We commonly justify what the Bible has stated as sin. Christian couples sleep together before marriage, yet ask God to bless their relationship. Christian friends openly gossip and slander one another. Christian wives harbor bitterness and unforgiveness for an offense committed decades ago. Christian women unabashedly read "mommy porn," justifying the explicit sex scenes because of the seemingly redemptive elements. *It's a story about healing and about love. It gives you ideas that can revive your sex life. They end up getting married in the third book, so it's all okay.*

People sometimes say that it is "old fashioned" to define morality based on the Bible, but nothing is more "old fashioned" than wanting to define right and wrong for ourselves. Relative morality isn't "progressive"—it's ancient!

Way back in the garden of Eden, Satan planted doubt in Eve's mind about God's standard, about the consequences of sin, and about God's goodness. He's doing the same thing today through the popularity of entertainment like *Fifty Shades.*

Satan's greatest assault is to cast doubt on God's motive. He told Eve, "God doesn't really care about you. He wants to keep you in bondage. He knows that if you eat from the tree, you'll be wise like He is. You can't trust Him!"

Satan whispers these lies about sexual standards too. He

paints the "good girl" as missing out on life and the sexual immoral woman as the mature, fulfilled one. Is he right? Is the woman who follows God's standards really missing out?

John Piper states our problem is not that we like pleasure too much, but that we settle for too little.[3] Now that's a thought! Piper wasn't the only great thinker or the first to suggest this paradox. C. S. Lewis diagnosed the human race as "far too easily pleased." He wrote:

> We are half-hearted creatures, fooling about with drink and sex and ambition when infinite joy is offered us, like an ignorant child who wants to go on making mud pies in a slum because he cannot imagine what is meant by the offer of a holiday at the sea.[4]

As you consider your own temptations with sexuality, do they occur because your drive to experience pleasure is too great or because you settle for a cheap version of satisfaction? We must realize that every choice to compromise sexually is more than a moral failure... it is a choice away from the ultimate joy and pleasure for which we were created.

Do you really believe that sex before marriage, pornography, and sexual perversion are bringing pleasure to people? Is there great joy among those who feel "free" to experiment with bondage, online sex, and bisexuality? Is God trying to keep men and women from great joy and deep sexual satisfaction?

God is the greatest proponent of your pleasure—not the

pleasure that is sweet for a season, but the deep, profound satisfaction that only grows sweeter with time.

If you find yourself caught in a trap of counterfeit intimacy (whether porn, erotica, online sexual chat rooms, or any other form), *please* tell someone! You are not alone in your struggle. God offers forgiveness and freedom, but you must begin by being honest with your situation.[5]

# Is MASTURBATION a SIN?

# 18

This is probably the most personal and frequently asked question I get from both married and single women. It's a tough one to answer because the Bible doesn't address it and I also understand the amount of angst it causes women. I could take the easy road and just say, "If in doubt, don't do it." The fact is that many Christian women masturbate and feel horribly guilty about it. I've met women who feel more shame about masturbation than they do about having an adulterous affair, yet the Bible is silent on the issue of masturbation and says a whole lot about adultery.

Masturbation is a complicated issue that doesn't lend to a clear black-and-white answer. I want to be realistic about the struggle without giving freedom that God perhaps hasn't given.

### Let's start with the basics

At a purely biological level, masturbation isn't that much different than other things we do with our bodies. Little boys and girls quickly discover that their "private parts" feel really good to touch. As children grow, wise parents gently teach that touching some places of our bodies isn't appropriate to do in public.

While there is nothing inherently wrong with touching yourself to experience pleasure, masturbation becomes a moral issue because it involves sexuality. Sexuality has intrinsic moral and spiritual implications. As I've written earlier, every sexual choice is also a spiritual choice. Does that mean that masturbation is always wrong? I'm not convinced the answer is an automatic "yes" or "no." When the Bible doesn't give clear instruction on an issue, we look for principles to apply in our search for wisdom. Based on biblical principles, here are a few questions that can help you evaluate the issue given your personal circumstances.

### *What are you thinking about?*

While masturbation itself isn't addressed in the Bible, we know that thinking lustfully about someone you aren't married to is sinful (see 1 Thessalonians 4:3–5). Most women masturbate only when they are thinking about or looking at something sexual. Sexual fantasies about someone you are not married to are, as Jesus stated, "adultery of the heart."

> "But I say, anyone who even looks at a woman [or man] with lust has already committed adultery with her in his heart." (Matthew 5:28 NLT)

If you are single, fantasizing even about some fictional sexy guy is promoting lustful thoughts. If you're married and fantasizing about another man, you are violating, in your mind and heart, your promise to give yourself sexually only to your husband. On the other hand, there is nothing wrong with a married woman fantasizing about her own husband. The Song of Songs records the bride doing exactly that!

### *What is your motive?*

The Bible makes it clear that God is very concerned about our motives. For example, giving money to your church might be a wonderful act of worship or an empty gesture, depending upon the attitude of your heart. The same can be true of our sexual choices.

Sexuality was created to draw us into relationships. The hormones that flow through a young teenager's body awaken her desire to seek intimacy even if sexual intimacy isn't a biblical option for many years. The goal of masturbation is to bring yourself pleasure and relief of sexual tension, typically outside of relationship. For this reason, some believe that masturbation is inherently selfish, misusing the gift of sex. While that may be the case, I don't think it is always so cut and dried.

Many women learned (or were even taught) to masturbate at very young ages. This is particularly true of those who have been sexually violated and have been "sexualized" at a young age. While I wouldn't recommend masturbation, I also don't think we should add to the shame that women feel about their sexuality. Just like men have "wet dreams," many women masturbate and orgasm in their sleep. Single women are sexual. Even those who are committed to purity in mind and body have sexual hormones, dreams, and thoughts that impact their body.

There are some Christian leaders working with singles who believe that masturbation may be a way to stay sexually pure until marriage. While I would be very cautious to give that advice, I recognize that for some, masturbation is a way of channeling sexual urges away from the temptations to have sex. It's possible for the motive of masturbation to be for purity and a form of exercising self-control.

The question of motive is also important for a married woman. There is a huge difference between a selfish wife who masturbates because she is withholding sex from her husband and a wife who masturbates for the purpose of building intimacy with her husband. Consider, for example, a wife who is separated from her husband because of travel, deployment, or long-term illness. She wants to focus on her husband and channel her sexual urges toward him.

Masturbation can even be beneficial for a married couple in cases of sexual dysfunction. A very common form of sex therapy called "sensate focus" helps a woman pay attention to how she responds to sexual touch, first by touching herself and then by guiding her husband's hand as he touches her. This can be an important step in healing, particularly for women who have experienced sexual trauma that triggers anxiety at sexual touch.

### *Is it mastering you? (No pun intended)*

The apostle Paul stated that "I will not be mastered by anything" (1 Corinthians 6:12). In other words, we shouldn't be controlled or addicted to anything. This applies to food, shopping, and also to masturbation. Women may use masturbation as a way to escape from boredom, loneliness, depression, pain, and stress. We learn at a young age to soothe ourselves with something that feels good. Some ways of coping with stress and boredom are clearly unhealthy, like drinking alcohol or cutting. Other forms of coping are destructive because they abuse an inherently good thing. For example, food is a wonderful gift, but a binge on ice cream and Doritos because you are lonely is abusing that gift. The same is true of sexuality. The neurochemicals released during sex and orgasm reduce stress, help you sleep, and make you feel at peace. However, having sex outside of marriage or habitually masturbating is an abuse of the body's natural response to sex.

Some singles find that when they get married they can't be aroused by their spouse because of habitual masturbation before marriage. Your body can get so used to the sensation you create for yourself that you can't respond to your husband's touch.

If you are masturbating on a regular basis or use it to deal with negative emotions, I'd encourage you to find other means of coping. God gave us healthy ways to release the chemicals in the body that bring peace and contentment. Prayer, meditation, exercise, talking to a friend, or creating something artistic might take more work, but they are alternatives to falling into an addictive cycle.

### *Am I honoring God with my body?*

"Don't you realize that your body is the temple of the Holy Spirit, who lives in you and was given to you by God? You do not belong to yourself, for God bought you with a high price. So you must honor God with your body" (1 Corinthians 6:19–20 NLT).

This verse can bring conviction regarding a lot of choices we make with our body, but it was written in the context of sexuality. If there is a "gold standard" question to ask, this is it. The answer to whether you're glorifying God in your body may be "yes," but in other situations the answer is clearly "no" for the same behavior.

I have great respect for women (married and single) who want to honor God with their sexuality. I believe masturbation is an issue that each woman has to ask the Lord about. When God wanted to be clear about something, He inspired direct teaching in Scripture. The Bible is silent on masturbation, although God has given us much guidance on the purpose of sexuality and the call to pursue purity. What God *did* state definitely is that He wants to give you His wisdom. "If any of you lacks wisdom, you should ask God, who gives generously to all without finding fault, and it will be given to you" (James 1:5).

God is the High Priest who understands our questions and struggles. Even in this most intimate (and perhaps embarrassing) issue, don't be afraid to pour out your heart to Him and ask for His specific direction and wisdom.

Can I be
GODLY
and
GAY?

# 19

This question is a powder keg—an extremely sensitive issue. If you have homosexual or bisexual tendencies, this is not just a theological debate, but speaks to the core of how you see yourself and how God views you.

The homosexual conversation impacts not just those who identify themselves as LGBT (Lesbian, Gay, Bisexual, Transgender), but all of us. Regardless of whether you can relate with this struggle, you will have to sort through your own views on the topic. If you do not already, you will have a good friend or family member who is gay. You will have to make decisions about whether to go to a same-sex wedding, whether to have your daughter and her partner over for dinner, and whether to attend a church with a gay pastor.

Within the last decade, the Christian opinion on homosexuality has gone through a drastic turnaround. There has been no new scientific or theological discovery; many people have changed their minds about what they believe.

In today's changing world, stating that homosexuality is anything but an acceptable lifestyle, approved by God, is seen as unloving, judgmental, hateful, and in some places, criminal. One of the most wonderful and difficult things about being a Christ-follower is that God doesn't change. "Jesus Christ is the same yesterday and today and forever" (Hebrews 13:8). Although our interpretations and emphasis of biblical teaching are fickle, the Word of God is a solid foundation for Christians living two thousand years ago and for Christians living today. I take great comfort in knowing that God's teachings are true and unchanging, but it also becomes difficult to stand on those truths when the cultural tide so quickly turns against them.

### *The Bible and homosexuality*

If you have read much on this issue, you know that there have been valiant attempts to re-interpret the six passages that specifically address homosexuality (Genesis 19, Leviticus 18:22, Leviticus 20:13, Romans 1:24–27, 1 Corinthians 6:9, 1 Timothy 1:10). Advocates of homosexuality write off the Old Testament passages as obsolete for New Testament Christians. They also interpret the sins of Sodom and Gomorrah as violence and lack of hospitality rather than homosexual behavior. Speaking of New Testament passages, they claim that Paul and early church leaders didn't understand sexual orientation. The prohibitions against homosexual behavior, they say, relates to orgies and homosexual acts committed by heterosexuals.

The concept of a homosexual orientation was first suggested in the 1890s, ironically around the same time as the field of psychology was established. However, we can assume that men and women in biblical times still struggled with sexual orientation and gender identity even if they didn't have the words to label them. Although the classification of LGBT issues has only recently evolved, human nature hasn't changed. The Bible's teaching on sexual immorality and homosexuality addresses human brokenness and sin, no matter what we choose to call it.

Although I am not a theologian, I have studied the arguments on both sides. The Bible is clear that "at the beginning of creation God made them male and female. For this reason a man will leave his father and mother and be united to his wife, and the two will become one flesh" (Mark 10:6–7).

I would encourage you to research the issue for yourself. Here are a few articles that explain why recent attempts to biblically justify the gay lifestyle are misguided: "Why *God and the Gay Christian* Is Wrong about the Bible and Same-Sex Relationships" by Christopher Yuan[1] and "God, the Gospel, and the Gay Challenge—A Response to Matthew Vines" by Al Mohler.[2]

Proverbs reminds us that "the fear of the Lord is the beginning of knowledge" (Proverbs 1:7). Whenever we endeavor to know or understand something, our approach must be rooted in who God is. His sovereignty is the anchor that keeps us from drifting into foolishness. Our view of God, even among some Christian scholars, has sunk so low that our wisdom has become foolishness on many sexual issues, including homosexuality.

We will never resolve the "godly and gay" question by looking inwardly at who we are, only by looking upward at who He is.

### God's compassion and holiness never cancel each other out.

When I hear the debate about God and the LGBT lifestyle, it sometimes sounds like an argument over whether God's holiness or love is more important. Some say, "A compassionate God wants us to love and enjoy the full expression of sexual love. He would never say that a gay person couldn't experience that." On the other side of the issue, God's holiness and call for us to be pure can be expressed without grace or compassion: "Gay men and women just need to choose to follow God and that's the end of it."

We are such limited moral and spiritual creatures that we can't grasp how God could be both loving and morally perfect. We reason that surely He must compromise one attribute to allow for the other.

The truth about God is that He is absolutely holy *and* unconditionally loving. We can never understand God's love if we don't also embrace His holiness. In *My Utmost for His Highest* Oswald Chambers wrote, "Anything that belittles or obliterates the holiness of God by a false view of the love of God is untrue to the revelation given by Jesus Christ."[3]

Many well-meaning Christians excuse and condone sin in the spirit of trying to show the love of God. I call these "sins of compassion." Instead of a worshiping a God of compassion, we have made compassion a god unto itself, ignoring God's call to righteousness and holiness.

I can be moved by compassion to excuse and condone almost any sin. My compassion for someone in chronic pain can justify taking a life. Compassion for a pregnant teenager who has her life ahead of her can cause me to excuse abortion. My compassion for a woman in a loveless marriage can move me to understand an affair. And my compassion for a gay man or lesbian can lead me to explain away or ignore God's standard for sexual love.

God's love is limitless, but it does have boundaries. His compassion never cancels out His truth and holiness.

Remember the rich young ruler who asked Jesus what he must do to inherit eternal life? Jesus told him the standard, to forsake his wealth and follow Him. When the young man walked away from Jesus, our Savior was grieved, but He did not change the standard of righteousness.

There have been generations of Christians who have taught the holiness and wrath of God, excluding His great love and compassion. Now, we live in a generation that has done the opposite—exalting God's love and mercy, but largely ignoring His holiness. I believe this is the primary reason for the drastic shift in the church's position on the gay issue.

God is compassionate and loving and commands us to be the same. However, compassion has never meant changing the standards of God's call for each of us to "be holy because I, the Lord Your God, am holy" (Leviticus 19:2).

*God is able to deliver from sin
and heal us from brokenness.*

Few Christians who embrace homosexuality believe that it was part of God's original perfect design—that before the fall, God created some of us to be gay or lesbian or bisexual. Just look at the way our anatomy fits together, male and female. Consider that in the creation account in Genesis, God created Eve to "complete" Adam and that together they represent the image of God.

This means that homosexuality represents a fallen world—sin and brokenness—just as our propensity toward addiction, gluttony, pride, hatred, and selfishness does. If there is a "gay gene," we could argue that there is also a promiscuity gene and anger gene. To accept homosexuality as a normal expression of God's design is to say that God is okay with us living *within* our brokenness, instead of seeking Him *through* that brokenness.

At its core, embracing the LGBT lifestyle as acceptable and even godly implies a belief that God is either unable or unwilling to redeem this particular brokenness in an individual's life. While God rescues us from other sins, He is not quite wise enough to solve the complicated issues involving homosexuality.

Perhaps the confusion comes because we have dictated to God what "healing" from homosexuality should look like. If a woman has sexual desire for another woman, healing must mean she becomes attracted to men, gets married to a caring Christian husband, has a houseful of children, and lives happily ever after in her feminine, suburban home. If that doesn't happen or a woman superficially embraces these trappings simply to prove that she's redeemed, God's healing seems to have failed.

God is God. How He deals with each of us in our sin and brokenness is His business. Healing and redemption usually don't mean our messy lives are now wrapped in a nice, neat bow. The apostle Paul alluded to the messiness of his own redemption. Throughout his Christian walk, he lived with a "thorn in the flesh, a messenger from Satan" that God refused to remove in order to keep Paul dependent upon God's grace. Paul longed for heaven so he could be free from this fallen world and the struggle of his own flesh.

Sometimes God delivers us from our brokenness and other times He strengthens us through it. The bottom line is this: God's power *is sufficient* in your weakness, even if that weakness happens to be a pull toward homosexuality.

### *There is a difference between homosexual urges and homosexual actions.*

Every one of us can identify with specific temptations that plague us. The draw to pornography seems too strong to resist or you just can't stop sleeping with your boyfriend. Or maybe you tend to lie more naturally than telling the truth or you secretly love a juicy morsel of gossip.

We rarely identify ourselves based on our temptations. I hear no arguments about the legitimacy of living life as a liar or fornicator. Yet homosexuality seems to be integrated into identity. You are not defined as someone who struggles with same-sex attraction but as a lesbian. Because of this, separating the action from the identity is often difficult.

Unfortunately, many men and women who have homosexual thoughts and urges feel condemned and dirty simply for having the struggle. Religious institutions have added to that shame by categorizing homosexual urges as more repugnant than any other temptation. In an effort to correct that prejudice, the pendulum has swung to giving spiritual license to those who actively pursue an LGBT lifestyle.

A person is not sinful because they have homosexual thoughts or desires. In fact, we all are predisposed by biology and/or early environment to grapple with something—depression, alcoholism, rage, habitual masturbation, bulimia. But there's a difference between normalizing a struggle and legitimizing the actions the struggle leads to.

Many godly men and women continue to wrestle with homosexual thoughts and urges, but have committed themselves to saying "no" to acting out on those desires. Living a godly life doesn't mean embracing sin. Nor does it mean one is never tempted. It means accepting God's compassionate love while also relying on His strength to pursue holiness.

The black and white words written in this book can never capture the pain you may have endured related to your own or a loved one's experience with homosexuality. My intention is not to add to that pain, but to remind you of how great our God is. I pray that God's exceedingly great love will surround you as you seek Him in the midst of your circumstances.

How do I
REBUILD TRUST
after a
BETRAYAL?

# 20

There is no pain like discovering that your husband has been unfaithful. It's as if your whole world has been shattered. You doubt your instincts because you have been fooled. You make vows to never trust again because old vows have been broken.

Based on God's Word, there is no greater offense in marriage than unfaithfulness. In fact, it is one of the only reasons that God allows for divorce—it's that serious! I've seen some couples who try to quickly move on and forget the whole matter. I think this is a mistake. While a marriage can certainly recover from betrayal, it is not a quick and painless process. Something precious has been broken and needs to be rebuilt.

### Does God understand my pain?

One of the biggest mistakes we make is trying to function in marriage without truly understanding the primary reason God created it in the first place. Marriage is not just a place to raise children or an agreement to make sure we are not lonely. It is a covenant that represents the promise of love God has made to His people.

Navigating the challenges of marriage—and the betrayal of infidelity—without understanding the larger meaning of God's covenant is kind of like putting together a puzzle without the picture on the box. Attempting to fit together a thousand tiny pieces into a picture is difficult enough, but imagine doing so without knowing what the final product is supposed to look like. How in the world can you begin to create a picture out of such chaos?

Marriage was never supposed to be about creating a love that is brand new; instead, it asks us to discover and replicate God's love that has existed since the garden of Eden. When I put together a puzzle, I constantly refer to the picture on the box. I scrupulously study each piece to discern where it fits within the whole picture. I think this is critical to navigating the waters of restoring broken trust.

God experienced unfaithfulness and infidelity with His chosen people—first the nation of Israel, and now those who are followers of Jesus. God often refers to the worship of other gods or idols as "adultery." Our hearts are to be pledged completely and totally to the Lord in the same way that a husband and wife promise to keep themselves for each other. In a very personal sense, God understands your pain.

### *Beyond "I'm sorry"*

Just as God extends forgiveness to us, He also asks us to extend forgiveness to someone who has betrayed us—even an unfaithful spouse. However, Jesus' forgiveness in our life isn't a reality until we are honest about our sin. "If we claim to be without sin, we deceive ourselves and the truth is not in us. If we confess our sins, he is faithful and just and will forgive us our sins and purify us from all unrighteousness" (1 John 1:8–9).

Is your husband repentant? Is he sorry because he got caught or does he truly understand the harm his infidelity has done? While God is always willing to reconcile with us, He doesn't offer "cheap forgiveness." In addition to saying, "I'm sorry!" God asks us to turn from our sin and to walk "in fellowship" with Him. The same is a requirement when trust in marriage has been broken.

God has the benefit of being able to see into our hearts. Since you can't look into your husband's heart to measure the sincerity of his remorse, it will take time and patience to begin to trust again. The shockwaves of a betrayal can reverberate for months, even years after the fact. This means that you may need to grapple with forgiveness and trust issues on an ongoing basis as they arise.

### *How much should I know?*

This is a critical question in the process of recovering from a betrayal. Some women feel like they need to know everything—

what he saw, what they did, and so on. Some counselors believe that when trust has been violated, you have a right to ask any and every question. After all, how can you rebuild trust if he is withholding information about what he's done?

While I agree that there should be no secrets, I've also found that knowing details can be a roadblock to rebuilding intimacy. In the wake of broken trust, you may feel an incessant need to know things that you wish you didn't know ten years down the road. It is very important to have a counselor help you and your husband sort through what detail is necessary for healing and what may create even more trauma. If information is withheld, it should always be for this reason, not because "I don't have to tell you that."

My friend Jill Savage is a godly woman whom I greatly respect. She and her husband Mark have walked through the process of rebuilding trust after infidelity. She speaks with wisdom and from experience:

> *As hard as it is for me to share about my husband's infidelity, it's my privilege to share how hard my husband worked to reestablish his integrity in our relationship. Mark committed to answer any question I asked.*
>
> *Sometimes he answered the same questions over and over again when I asked them from a slightly different angle. He was never exasperated by my need to know. He never exclaimed, "Can we stop now? I've apologized. When can we put this behind us?"*

*In the beginning, I asked dozens of questions each day. As time went on, my questions decreased to several times a week. Now we're three years out. Questions still arise, but they're no more than once a month, even just a few times a year. And Mark still answers them with patience and kindness.*

*As the one who was betrayed, I also had a responsibility in rebuilding trust. I intentionally chose not to ask particular questions, knowing the answers simply wouldn't help. I also committed to never throw my husband's choices in his face. I've learned that the purpose of asking questions should be to seek understanding, not indictment.*

*We have learned to ask healthy questions like, "How did that make you feel?" or "You're very quiet tonight. What's going on inside your head and your heart?" These questions bring thoughts and feelings into the light rather than keeping them in the dark crevices of our minds, where Satan often does his nastiest work.*[1]

### Rebuilding what was destroyed

God places such a high premium on sexual fidelity in marriage because He knows the level of vulnerability and trust a covenant requires. If your husband has been unfaithful, how can you know for certain he will never be unfaithful again? Choosing to love another person always involves an act of faith, hoping for what we cannot be certain about. However, no marriage can be based on "blind faith." In a marriage relationship, you and your husband owe it to each other to demonstrate a commitment to fidelity. This is particularly true if he has been unfaithful in the past.

Working with your counselor, you and your husband need to build safeguards or "hedges" around your marriage to protect against another betrayal. For example, do you have access to each other's cellphones and email accounts? Obviously, you could go overboard checking up on your husband, fueling an atmosphere of distrust and even paranoia. But in the wake of an affair, it is reasonable for you to expect a greater level of accountability in order to rebuild trust.

You also need to explore what led to the affair in the first place. In many cases, affairs happen because there are cracks in the marriage. Perhaps you and your spouse drifted apart, stopped communicating, and left each other lonely in the process. Maybe there were unresolved issues related to finances, sex, or parenting. Sometimes, an individual may have emotional problems such as past sexual abuse or bipolar disorder that lead to an increased likelihood of infidelity. Work with your counselor to identify what made your marriage vulnerable to the affair initially, then come up with practical ways to strengthen those weak areas.

I've met many couples who, like Mark and Jill Savage, testify to the healing power of forgiveness and restoration after betrayal. In the wake of their own healing journey, Gary and Mona Shriver started Hope and Healing ministries to help couples recover from sexual unfaithfulness.[2] Nothing is beyond God's redemption when a man and women are humble and willing to depend upon Him. However, rebuilding a marriage takes two people.

As complicated as the Bible can seem, it really is the ultimate love story. God loved us even when we were unfaithful to Him. In some cases, as with the prophet Hosea, God asked certain individuals to stay married even in spite of blatant betrayal. This may not have seemed like wise marriage advice, but God's greater purpose was to help us grasp His unfailing love. He is faithful even when we are not. Whether or not your marriage can be restored, God asks you to be faithful to Him through it all. God can be exalted and glorified through you in every situation—whether that means a restored marriage or you walking faithfully through the trial of a broken marriage.

Does
FORGIVENESS
mean I'll be
HURT AGAIN
❧ ? ❧

# 21

I often get asked questions about forgiveness from women who have been betrayed or violated by someone close to them. A husband is repeatedly unfaithful or a relative is abusive. The Bible's teaching on forgiveness seems to suggest that we continually put ourselves in risky situations. Yes, there is a time to "turn the other cheek," but there is also a time to wisely set healthy boundaries.

If trust has been broken in your marriage, please read Question #20 before reading this one. Because marriage is a sacred covenant, we are obligated to seek restoration as far as it depends upon us. Yes, marriages fall apart because of betrayal and a "hard heart." But there are many marriages that have been reconciled, rebuilt, and restored even after the devastation of broken vows.

When you have been deeply hurt and betrayed by someone, restoring that relationship can be very complicated. While the Bible is clear that we are always to forgive people who harm us, forgiveness doesn't necessarily mean that we go back to acting as if nothing ever happened. A severe offense or a pattern of abusive behavior breaks trust, and a relationship can't be close unless trust is rebuilt.

The Bible gives a very practical example of a godly man in an abusive relationship who had a forgiving heart but also kept his distance. The relationship I'm referring to is David and King Saul.

King Saul was not in his right mind. His mentality was so twisted by jealousy and rage toward David, that he was determined to kill him. While Saul and his men hunted down David, David hid, calling on the Lord for protection. In fact, many of the most beautiful Psalms were written as David hid from Saul.

A few times, the Lord put David in a position in which he could get rid of Saul once and for all. David's friends encouraged him to kill Saul, which many would have said he was justified in doing. But David had a sensitive heart toward the Lord and refused to harm Saul. Instead, he extended mercy and showed humility.

Here's what we can learn from David. He had every reason to seek revenge, but trusted God to carry out judgment against his enemy. He said, "May the Lord judge between you and me. And may the Lord avenge the wrongs you have done to me, but my hand will not touch you" (1 Samuel 24:12).

Saul responded to David's kindness with repentance. The great king of Israel wept aloud and admitted, "You are more righteous than I . . . You have treated me well but I have treated you badly." Saul confessed to David, "I have sinned" (1 Samuel 24:17). Then he offered to restore the relationship with David, "Come back, David my son. Because you considered my life precious today, I will not try to harm you again. Surely I have acted like a fool and have been terribly wrong" (1 Samuel 26:21).

Even so, David did not trust Saul. He had seen such remorse in him before, only to find himself in the crosshairs once again. The Bible says that "David went on his way, and Saul returned home" (1 Samuel 26:25).

Jesus told us to always forgive. This means that like David, we don't harbor bitterness in our hearts toward someone who has harmed us. Instead of taking revenge, we leave judgment to God. However, forgiveness doesn't always mean the relationship is restored. Reconciliation requires genuine repentance and the desire to rebuild trust. I've seen many amazing stories of marriages, friendships, and family relationships completely restored after a grievous betrayal. But other times, repentance is absent or shallow, and trust cannot be rebuilt.

The biblical story of Joseph and his brothers gives us a vivid account of betrayal and reconciliation. Out of jealousy, Joseph's brothers wanted to kill him, and sold him into slavery. That's a pretty serious betrayal! About twenty years later, Joseph's brothers came to Egypt to buy food when Israel was suffering a terrible famine. They unknowingly met Joseph, who as one of Pharaoh's highest officials held all the power—the power of life and death. Before Joseph revealed his identity, he tested his brothers to see if they were still malicious and jealous, or if their hearts had softened over the many years of their separation. While Joseph was open to restoration, he didn't trust his brothers until he knew that God had changed their hearts.

Both David and Joseph were godly men who acted with wisdom. Even Jesus showed love and compassion to all men, but did not always trust Himself to some people because He knew what was in their hearts (John 2:24). Likewise, we are called to be clothed with love, forgiveness, and compassion and to be open to restoration. However, wisdom dictates that we use discernment, knowing that sometimes it is best to love from a distance.

# WHAT
## *if*
# I DON'T
## *like*
# SEX?

# 22

I hate sex. It makes me angry to hear you even suggest that I'm supposed to be enjoying it. I've been married twenty-three years and have never enjoyed it. Frankly, I do it because I'm supposed to."

I hear from women like this one quite often. They feel ripped off, gypped out of something that they were supposed to enjoy. The message that sex is a gift from God sounds like an insult. Instead, they view sex as a gift that they must grudgingly give to their husband.

To some degree, that describes my feeling for many years of my marriage. No, I didn't hate sex, but I certainly dreaded it. As a woman who longed to be a godly wife, I determined before the Lord that I would meet my husband's needs. Although God was probably pleased with that attitude, it didn't represent the healing He wanted to do in my heart and in my marriage.

I want to share a few things God has taught me (and is still teaching me!) on this journey. I know that every woman's story is different; I am not offering a simplistic formula that will guarantee a miracle in your bedroom. However, I do believe God is able to bring healing into every woman's heart.

### Address the obstacles

Some want to have it every three hours and others once a week, but men almost universally find sex pleasurable—as we have already discussed. This is not true for some women. Female sexuality is far more complicated, providing the opportunity for more barriers to pleasure. Obstacles to sexual pleasure typically fall in three categories: physical, relational, and emotional.

### Physical

The female sexual response involves many functions of the body, including the endocrine, circulatory, skeletal, muscular, and reproductive systems. That means a lot can go wrong. For example, an underactive thyroid can destroy sexual desire and sexual response. An imbalance of hormones will do the same. Medications like antidepressants and even decongestants may affect sexual function.

Jennifer Smith's book *The Unveiled Wife* chronicles her journey through years of sexual pain in marriage. One day, she and her husband researched a hunch to find that an acne soap she had been using contained an ingredient that disrupted hormone balance. A week after she stopped using the cream, her sexual functioning immediately improved.[1]

Physical obstacles to sexual pleasure may be difficult to diagnose, partly because physical pain and lack of pleasure can also have psychological roots. Don't just give up after a doctor can't answer your questions. Search for the answer. Find the right doctor, midwife, physician's assistant, or nurse practitioner who understands sexual functions and disorders.

While most women resign themselves to a "broken" sex life, others relentlessly pursue a solution. My friend Kathy Cordell couldn't have sexual intercourse with her husband for over a decade. Her doctor gave her the advice to "have a drink of wine and just relax." Instead of solving the problem, this led to a substance addiction. Kathy's counselor challenged her to research a condition called vaginismus that causes pain during sex. Kathy found that some women have a learned fear response to intercourse, causing the vaginal muscles to tighten. In the wake of her own healing, Kathy now helps women who have this condition through the emotional, spiritual, and physical aspects of healing.[2]

Like Kathy, don't just resign yourself to painful sex or a lack of pleasure. Be tenacious in prayer and in seeking a solution.

### Relational

You can have a great marriage and a rotten sex life. However, the quality of your marriage is the foundation upon which you build sexual intimacy. Do you trust your husband in the bedroom? Is he sensitive to your needs? Do you communicate with

185

each other about sex? Do you have secrets, bitterness, or unfor-giveness between you?

Sara is one of those women who hated sex. Over the eleven years of their marriage, it was a demand her husband, Jake, made several times a week. He never asked if she would like to have sex—he assumed it was his God-given right as a married man. Sex made Sara feel like an object. She wondered if Jake even cared that it was *her* body he was caressing.

Joyce and Ben had a different barrier between them. Through-out their nineteen years of marriage, Ben had dabbled with porn off and on. Although Ben confessed to a one-night stand on a business trip, the matter was quickly swept under the rug as if it never happened. Joyce felt like a part of her heart was dead. She consented to share her body with Ben, but kept her heart closed to intimacy.

Sexuality taps into some of our greatest areas of vulnerability. In the daily routine of marriage, we often don't stop to consider how we've been wounded in marriage or why we don't trust the man who sleeps beside us every night. However, until these issues are surfaced and addressed, physical pleasure and freedom is unlikely to be a reality.

### Emotional

I believe the most common barriers to enjoying sex are emo-tional. Some women have a history of trauma or destructive choices that has paired sex with extremely negative and painful emotions.

Sex = shame
Sex = guilt
Sex = sin
Sex = exploitation
Sex = I'm only good for one thing

Putting a wedding ring on and saying vows in a church doesn't erase those messages. The emotional trauma connected to sexual brokenness is often so deep that you may not even be aware of it. Many women don't remember the details of childhood sexual abuse until adulthood. They may simply carry a vague sense of "something isn't right."

Other women have no history of sexual trauma or guilt from past mistakes, but still can't seem to enjoy sex. I meet women who have saved themselves for marriage, dreaming of the ecstasy that sex is supposed to promise. No matter how hard they try, they simply can't feel free to enjoy sex. The idea of trying something new brings panic and waves of disgust.

Because sex is such a private area of struggle, women often don't know where to go for help. They simply settle for frustration in this area of life. We live in a day and age in which help is readily available, even related to sexual problems. Yet, reaching out to a counselor or even buying a book on the topic is frightening.

If you have sexual trauma in your past or events in your life marred by shame, the thought of talking through this pain may seem unbearable. Emotional wounds can be more painful than physical wounds, but you can't see them. It takes tremendous courage to seek help knowing that you will be sharing with someone else an area of your life marked by shame and sorrow. It may seem easier just to ignore the pain and move on in your marriage, but God is Jehovah Rapha, the One who invites you to healing.

### *Expose the lies*

Healing from physical, relational, and emotional barriers to sex takes work and effort. It begins with a commitment to identify them and address them. If you are tired of disappointment in the bedroom, your journey toward healing may mean overcoming a few commonly held lies about sex. These lies keep women from pursuing healing. They just assume, "This is as good as it's going to get. I guess I'm just not one of those women who will ever enjoy sex."

*Lie #1—God created sex primarily for a man's pleasure.* Because women believe this lie, they build sexual intimacy around a man's needs, having sex when and how he wants it. After years or decades of marriage, you may never have considered that your needs matter too! It is worth exploring how sex can be satisfying for you, and it is worth pursuing counseling to work through the pain of the past. Don't settle!

*Lie #2— It's not right for a godly woman to be sexual.* No one says this lie out loud, but a lot of women live by it. Sexual excitement is automatically linked with sexual immorality. Other women "punish" themselves for past sexual mistakes by not enjoying sex now in their marriage. They have bought the lie that to be sexual means to be sinful.

One reason why women have difficulty enjoying sexual pleasure is because they think they need to simply wait for it to happen. They don't realize that enjoying sex or having an orgasm requires their active participation. It's not going to happen if you are thinking about the mold growing on the shower curtain or your three year-old in the next room.

Most women report that they don't actually even want to have sex until they start thinking about it and anticipating it. When women view sex primarily as a wifely duty, they don't even consider that their own arousal is as important as his. A woman has her own mental and physical "pathway to pleasure" that may take time to discover and pursue.

As I mentioned earlier, Linda Dillow and I wrote a Bible study called *Passion Pursuit* (Moody Publishers) to help women understand God's design for passionate love in marriage. We have seen many women set free and enjoy sex even after decades of an unsatisfying sex life.

As obvious as it sounds, nothing will change if you change nothing. Just like your kitchen won't magically clean itself, your sexual struggles and wounds won't simply disappear one day.

No one can promise you that your sex drive will go from zero to sixty in ninety days. We live in a fallen world filled with disappointment and brokenness. But would you be willing to take one small step? That might be calling a counselor, going through the Bible study *Passion Pursuit,* or maybe even praying with your husband about your sex life. It takes effort, prayer, and courage to step into healing, but it's worth it!

How do I
MAKE TIME
— to —
MAKE LOVE
?

# 23

After a long day of taking care of three little boys, cooking, cleaning, and juggling work responsibilities, I had reached the "finish line." It was my time to rest. I ignored the subtle flirtations of my husband, Mike, hoping he would get the hint that I was not in the mood. As we were getting ready for bed, I changed into my pj's and he caught a "glimpse" of flesh. He looked at me amorously as if the act of changing my clothes was an invitation. I faced a fork in the road: would I "do my wifely duty" or tell Mike what I was really thinking? I responded with a compromise: "We can do it as long as I don't have to be awake."

If this had only happened once in a blue moon, our marriage could weather the storm. However, scenes like this one were regular occurrences during the busy years of babies and toddlers. I began to dread sex. Although I loved my husband, I resented that he wanted my body and was encroaching on my rare moments of free time.

I'm guessing that many young moms can relate to this scenario. The number one barrier to sexual enjoyment for women is a lack of time and energy. Men often don't understand the mammoth endeavor it can be to switch from "mommy mode" to "lover," especially when a screaming child is in the next room and dirty dishes are piled in the sink. Who has time for sex?

It was during these busy years that I wrote a book called *No More Headaches.* How ironic that I could find time to write a book about sex but not find the time to actually engage in it! I desperately wanted to discover the secret to getting past the barriers that kept our sex life at best mediocre.

My boys are now in their teen years. There are still challenges, including the fact that teenagers NEVER go to bed and they don't fall for the whole "Mom and Dad are just wrestling" line. But God has taught me a lot about the importance of sex in marriage and how to make it happen, even in the busiest stage of your life.

### *Why you can't put sex on the back burner*

Study after study shows that sexual satisfaction and a healthy marriage go together. From a woman's perspective, we think, *Of course! If the marriage is good, the sex will be too.* Men have a different approach: "How could marriage be good without great sex?" According to recent research, the guys actually have a point.

Oxytocin is the powerful bonding hormone that flows through your body in mass quantities when you have a baby.

Oxytocin helps you to feel connected to your baby and helps you weather the crazy years of toddlerhood. The power of oxytocin makes your baby the most beautiful creature in the world to you. Women have varying levels of oxytocin running through their bodies at any given time. You may get a surge of it when you have an intimate conversation with a friend or when your husband gives you a backrub. Men are less endowed in the oxytocin department. Your husband will only have huge surges of the hormone at one time—after orgasm. Have you ever noticed that he acts more in love with you after sex? He thinks you are gorgeous with your hair sticking up and your morning breath. That's oxytocin!

I need my husband to be bonded with me. I need his attention and his help with the demands of children and life. God has designed a way for this to happen through sexual intercourse. It truly is how many men feel the closest to their wives. Understanding the power of the chemicals involved in sex has given me a new appreciation for how critical it is to the health of our marriage. When I sense tension between my husband and me I often think, *That man needs some oxytocin!*

I could give you many other reasons why sex is so powerful, important, and not to be neglected. One of them includes the positive impact endorphins (also released after sex) have on you. Regular sex lowers blood pressure, reduces stress, boosts immunity, burns calories, helps you sleep better, and even slows the aging process. Yet, even with all this information, it may seem like a monumental task to make sex a priority in your marriage.

You may have legitimate barriers to overcome like body image issues, deep conflict with your husband, broken trust, wounds from sexual trauma, or physical pain during sex. I don't want to make light of these painful circumstances, but often, great sex doesn't happen because it's simply not a priority.

### *Practical ways to make sex a reality during busy times*

Although you may never feel as tired as you do as a young mom, there will always be some reason to neglect sex in your marriage. Like anything else, it won't get better until you determine to change some things. Busy women find time to do what they deem important. They work out, go to Bible studies, volunteer in the classroom, and create elaborate scrapbooks. Is it time for you to make sex a priority? If so, here are some ways to make that happen.

**Schedule Sex**

This might sound like the most unromantic idea on the planet, but spontaneous sex rarely happens in the busy years of raising kids. You need time to get your mind and body prepared to be intimate with your husband. If you simply wait until bedtime, the chances of you both being ready with energy at the same time are slim to none. Then sex becomes an act of service for one of you. The goal is for you both to enjoy the intimacy and pleasure of great sex.

Couples "schedule sex" in different ways. Some actually put it on the calendar one to three times a week. Other couples agree that each of them will initiate at least once a week. My husband and I had a code word that he would use meaning, "Let's have sex sometime in the next twenty-four hours." Then I had the freedom to initiate within that time frame when it was good for me.

### Think about Sex

The bestselling book series *Fifty Shades of Grey* has proven one thing. Women want to think about sex and feel sexually stimulated when they do. I've heard from scores of Christian women who are eating up erotic books like *Fifty Shades* because reading about sex helps their sex life.

Please don't fall into the trap of erotica. It is pornography for women. Although it will initially stimulate you sexually, it will ultimately lead to distance between you and your husband. The greatest sex happens when we are naked in all ways. Porn and erotica cause you to share your body with your husband but stay "hidden" from him in your own secret fantasies.

A holy, erotic book called the Song of Songs gives a Christian woman permission to fantasize and think about being sexual with her husband in a way that honors God. When you understand the symbolism of the book, you will be surprised by how specific, steamy, and erotic this book is—and it's in the Bible! If you are married, God wants you to think about sex, but to keep your fantasies and thoughts geared only toward your husband. The brain is the most powerful sex organ, especially for women—learn how to use it to spice up your marriage.

**Pray about Sex**

Yes, you read right. God cares about your sex life. He understands the devastation of finding out your husband is looking at porn or has no interest in sex. He knows the pain of your sexual trauma. He even cares about your exhaustion or depression. As a clinical psychologist, I've worked with many women through such barriers. While counseling can be a step in healing, God is the ultimate Healer.

If your husband is willing, get on your knees together once a week and ask God to show you how to love each other sexually. Ask Him to help you work through the barriers that cause division between you.

There are a lot of great things you can give your kids. You may be sacrificing time and money to take them to play groups, sporting events, and music lessons. But remember this: none of these compare to the foundation of growing up in a home in which Mom and Dad love each other. Work hard at being a mom, but never at the expense of enjoying a thriving marriage.

How do we
FIGHT
= without =
HURTING
each other?

# 24

My husband, Mike, and I are very, very different. Early in our marriage, these differences created *a lot* of tensions. There were days when I wondered if we could make it with such divergent views on everything from money to parenting.

Mike and I are still very different. While that continues to create disagreement, we rarely fight anymore. We discovered a secret that has made our marriage immeasurably more enjoyable.

### *You can have conflict without fighting.*

Because we typically use the two words interchangeably, most couples don't know the difference between a *conflict* and a *fight*. Conflict in marriage is absolutely inevitable. Because you are two separate people with your own thoughts, desires, and beliefs, you will have conflict. Fighting, however, is optional.

A famous marriage researcher, Dr. John Gottman, discovered that one of the primary indications of whether or not a couple would stay together was how they handled conflict.[1] Please note: the difference wasn't *how much* conflict the couple had, but how they handled it. You and your husband may disagree about many things, but if you have the skills to resolve conflict without fighting, you can have a harmonious marriage.

When you think of the word *fight* you probably imagine a couple yelling and screaming at each other. However, you and your husband can "fight" without ever raising your voices. A couple can be fighting in their marriage when they become verbally aggressive, contemptuous, or withdrawn in marriage. I used to pride myself in not losing my temper like my Irish husband did. Then I realized that I was doing just as much damage with quiet sarcasm, an arrogant attitude, or giving him the cold shoulder for days.

It is never God's will for us to fight in marriage. We will most likely have some important and emotional conflicts, but those do not have to include fighting.

I want to share with you three primary differences between conflict and having a fight.

### *Conflicts are intentional and fights are impulsive.*

When Mike and I address a conflict, we are intentional about bringing up an issue that needs to be resolved. Sometimes that means that I've spent several days praying about the issue, thinking it through, and perhaps getting some perspective from a trusted friend.

A fight always begins with an impulsive reaction to how we are feeling. He said something insensitive or I did something that ticked Mike off, and away we go. When we get into a fight, it usually feels for one of us like we *have* to talk about it *right now*—not because it's urgent but because we can't control how we are feeling.

One of the greatest lessons we've learned is that almost all conflicts are more likely to be resolved if we give each other time to process, pray, and get perspective. As a young bride, I bought into the advice "Never go to bed angry." I took this to mean that we had to solve every problem before going to sleep. You know what I learned? Two in the morning is not a good time to talk through an issue.

Most important issues in a marriage don't have to be resolved today. You don't have to decide on what car to buy, where to send the kids to school, or how to pay the credit card bill. Although it may *feel* like you need resolution, find your own peace in bringing the issue before the Lord before seeking peace with your spouse.

### *Fights are rooted in fear and pride while conflict requires humility.*

When you and your spouse are engaged in fighting, you both want to win. You are convinced that you have the better argument, are more justified in your anger than he is or you want to hurt him as much as he hurt you.

Fights typically end with a perceived winner and loser. Someone got the last word or overpowers the other one.

The goal of conflict is to end up on the same page. Conflict isn't motivated by getting your way or proving your point. The goal is to become like-minded and understanding each other at a deeper level. Even if you and your husband will never see an issue exactly the same, through conflict, you can gain an appreciation for each other's perspective.

One of the most powerful things you can do to switch a fight into a healthy conflict is to take a step toward humility. Although I'm the psychologist, my husband is often better at practicing this than I am. When a fight begins to escalate, Mike will sometimes say something that demonstrates that he's not simply motivated to win.

"Juli, I don't want to fight with you. I love you! Remember that you and I are on the same team."

This immediately disarms me and helps me gain perspective.

Apologizing for your part of a misunderstanding is another way to demonstrate humility. "I'm sorry I said that the way I did. I didn't intend to hurt you, but what I said was uncalled for. Will you forgive me?"

While those words may be very difficult to utter in the heat of the battle, they will likely turn a contentious fight into a meaningful conflict. In essence, you are telling your husband, I care more about us than I care about getting my way.

### *Fighting is about the moment; conflict is about the marriage.*

One Sunday as Mike and I were driving with the kids to church, a yellow light prompted a fight between us. Mike was driving and I saw the light turn yellow when we were still a good distance away. I said something about how he should stop instead of stepping on the gas. This made Mike hesitate. His instincts would have certainly been to "squeeze the lemon." In his frustration, Mike swore.

Then I retorted with a snarky comment, "Really nice for you to swear in front of the boys because we will get to church a minute later. That's just a great example!"

Let's just say neither of us was in the mood to worship that morning.

Can you relate to this episode? Even with something as benign as a traffic light, you get pulled into the moment, and begin to do long-term damage to each other.

God is teaching me that I could win every argument and still lose my marriage. That perspective helps me practice the self-control and humility required to do conflict well.

### *Remember that conflicts won't simply disappear.*

I'm not suggesting that you walk away from an issue when you walk away from a fight. There are some conflicts you *must* walk through. Avoiding them is neither loving nor beneficial.

There are some conflicts in your marriage that will be really stressful. It's no fun to confront your husband on his porn use or decide as a couple whether or not to declare bankruptcy. These are very important issues that you need God's wisdom and grace to work through.

Switching from a pattern of fighting to healthy conflict means refusing to make your spouse the enemy and being patient to wait until the right time and setting to talk the issues through in a loving manner. Ask God to give you the wisdom you need to make this change in your heart and your marriage.

Why WOULDN'T GOD WANT ME to be HAPPY?

# 25

*God would never give someone sexual desires that He doesn't intend to fulfill.*

*God doesn't want me to stay in an unhappy marriage. He knows I'm miserable and would be happier with someone else.*

This kind of thinking pervades modern Christianity as it relates to sexuality. A woman who recently contacted me had this to say:

> I used to be an advocate for waiting to have sex until marriage, but as the years have gone by I no longer feel this way. I think it's all well and good for teens and those in their early twenties to strive for such a goal, but as someone who has recently entered her late twenties, it seems like an outdated and irrelevant idea to hold on to. I'm dating a Christian man right now, but who knows if we will have sex outside of marriage . . . I just know that waiting isn't something I'm personally interested in anymore.

I don't think most men and women doubt what the Bible says about sex. Instead, they find it in conflict with what they believe about God—that He is loving and wants the best for them. If a command of God seems to be outside of their best interest, they write it off with the assurance that a loving God would want them to be happy. Would God really want His followers to be miserable and lonely in their self-denial? In order to understand this dilemma, we need to reexamine two concepts we naturally take for granted: happiness and love.

### *What is happiness, anyway?*

Where did we get this idea that happiness comes from having everything we want in life? If you are a mom, you've seen it in your kids. Your daughter has been *begging* you nonstop for a toy she wants. One day, you surprise her with it, thinking that you've just won the mom of the year award. For about ten minutes, your daughter is ecstatic and grateful for the gift. Before the sun goes down, she's likely complaining or asking for the next greatest thing.

The happiness of getting what we want is fleeting. Whatever it is that you think God is keeping you from (great sex, a boyfriend, a happy marriage, freedom from a miserable marriage), if you go after it, your happiness will be very short-lived.

Interestingly, the secular world has concluded the same thing. There are people in poor countries who have literally nothing, but they are "happier" than we are. How can that be? One of the greatest ways to find happiness is to be grateful. The most thankful people, regardless of what they have, are the happiest. The apostle Paul shared his journey in discovering this: "I know how to get along with humble means, and I also know how to live in prosperity; in any and every circumstance I have learned the secret of being filled and going hungry, both of having abundance and suffering need. I can do all things through Him who strengthens me" (Philippians 4:12–13 NASB).

God doesn't want us to be happy in the childish "I just got a pony!" sense. He longs for His children to discover a deeper happiness that comes through fellowship with Him and a grateful heart. If you are in an unhappy season of life, would you be willing to take a challenge? For one month, keep a "Thankful Journal." Every day, journal a few paragraphs about what you are thankful for.

I recently had a conversation with a dear woman, Michele Cushatt, author of the book *Undone: The Story of Making Peace with an Unexpected Life*. Because of recurring tongue cancer, she has been through gruesome surgeries, chemotherapy, and radiation, and she had just recently had two-thirds of her tongue cut out. Michele explained that she is choosing to find joy. "I walked in here with two legs. I have two eyes that work and can see your face. I have ears that work that can hear your voice. Based on the life expectancy of many countries in the world, I'm already in the 'bonus' at 43. I can choose to focus on what I don't have, or I can choose to find joy in what I have."[1]

Does God want you be happy? He often doesn't allow us to

have what we demand because He longs to teach us an abiding happiness and joy that the world can never take away.

### *Exposing a heresy of love*

"That's heresy!" The phrase sounds like it's from some scene taking place centuries ago with Martin Luther or Galileo, but heresy is alive and well today. Heresy is any teaching or belief that stands against what is clearly stated in the Bible. John warned against heresies that deny the deity of Jesus or that proclaimed another way to the Father aside from trusting in Jesus. Even today, we must also be on guard for subtle heresies that sneak into our thinking.

A. W. Tozer stated, "When large numbers of adherents in the Christian churches come to believe that God is different from what He actually is, that concept becomes heresy of the most insidious and deadly kind!"[2]

Tozer taught that such heresy begins when we emphasize one attribute of God above all the other attributes. In other words, we can be holding to truths about God, but favoring certain truths to the point where we disregard the totality of God's character.

There is a significant danger in the modern trend to exclusively emphasize God's love. The Bible has much to say about God's love. In fact, God is love. Jesus told us that all of the prophets and the Law could be summed up in the commandment of love—loving God and loving others. Although there is obviously great importance placed on God's love, His love never cancels out His holiness, His justice, and His righteousness.

On the basis of His holiness and righteousness, this God of love will condemn people to hell. He has set out rules for holy living that are not to be taken lightly. He calls certain actions, thoughts, and lifestyles "sinful" and destructive.

As I teach in the arena of sexuality and marriage, the "heresy of love" is particularly evident. Many Christians make decisions on what God allows based on the belief that a loving God would want them to be happy and fulfilled. I've met with women who use this logic to justify sex outside of the covenant of marriage, having affairs, and using mommy porn. I remember meeting with one married woman who was convinced that God brought another man into her life because He knew she was suffering in a difficult marriage. She and her "lover" prayed together, read the Bible, all the while justifying their affair. This woman could find verses in the Bible to remind her of God's compassion and love. But was she simply skipping past the passages that demand holiness and self-denial?

God is the Father who waits for the prodigal to return. He is the Shepherd who leaves the flock to find the lost sheep. He is the merciful Savior who gave His life to cleanse our sin. He is the Man of Sorrows who is close to the brokenhearted. But let's not forget, He is the righteous Judge who will bring hidden things into the light. He is the God of wrath who destroys the wicked. He is the Spirit of Truth who rebukes and calls sinners to repentance. He is the Master who told His dearest friends to suffer and deny themselves for His sake. He is Holy!

### *By faith do you believe?*

Oswald Chambers wrote "Jesus Christ and He alone is able to satisfy the craving of the human heart to know the meaning of life. He enables men to understand that they have come into this life from a deep purpose in the heart of God; that the one thing they are here for it get readjusted to God and become His lovers."[3]

Do you believe that statement? Is it true that Jesus can satisfy your cravings more completely than any other pursuit in this world? If you were to live by that conviction, how would it change your approach to relationships and sexuality?

Hebrews 11:6 says, "And without faith it is impossible to please God, because anyone who comes to him must believe that he exists and that he rewards those who earnestly seek him." It takes faith to believe that God sees your decision to say "no" to immoral sex or to say "yes" to loving a difficult husband and that He will meet the desires of your heart.

The rewards of a godly life may not be Prince Charming waiting in the wings or happily ever after in your marriage. Sometimes God brings those gifts, but He never promised them. The spiritual blessings God gives His disciples are hard to see but impossible to deny. The apostle Peter described it this way, "Though you have not seen him, you love him; and even though you do not see him now, you believe in him and are filled with an inexpressible and glorious joy" (1 Peter 1:8).

How you live out your sexuality may seem like a very personal decision, but it also tells the world what you believe about God. Unfortunately, many Christians are modeling for the world a god that bears little resemblance to the Almighty One the Bible speaks of. As David Platt once said, "We are living a cross-less Christianity."[4] We want the promises of God without considering the cost of actually following Jesus.

My friend, it requires great faith living within our fallen world to believe that honoring God with every relationship and sexual choice is worthwhile. You may be teased, mocked, and have some lonely seasons. Even then, your loving Father is for your deepest joy.

The question is not about how much God loves you, but how much you love Him. Jesus said to His disciples and says to us today, "If you love me, keep my commands" (John 14:15). It is in loving Him and seeking Him that you will find your greatest happiness.

*When God stops giving us things, He brings us into the place where we can begin to understand Him. As long as we get from God everything we ask for, we never get to know Him, we look upon Him as a blessing-machine that has nothing to do with God's character or with our characters. It is not sufficient for us to say, "Oh yes, God is love." We have to know He is love. We have to struggle through until we do see He is love and justice. Then our prayer is answered.*[5]

# Final Thoughts

I wish I could have a cup of coffee with you right now. Throughout this book, I've shared a lot of thoughts about twenty-five questions. Now I'm wondering what you're thinking. What was helpful to you? What was painful? Was there something you read that made you mad or that you really disagree with? Do you have more questions that weren't addressed in this book?

The ministry Linda Dillow and I founded, Authentic Intimacy, isn't simply about *sex education*, it's about *sexual discipleship*. The goal isn't for you to read this book and move on with life, but to begin seeking the Lord and exploring truth in the most private issues in your life. We have a weekly radio show and podcast called "Java with Juli," online Bible studies, events, and a blog in partnership with *Today's Christian Woman*. You can find it all through our website at www.authenticintimacy.com.

While I'd love to connect you with the resources we have at Authentic Intimacy, I'm even more passionate about connecting you with the Lord Himself. There is no area of your life that He doesn't already know about. There is no sin too great or wound too deep for His redemption.

You and I can't have coffee today, but your Creator and Savior wants you to share what's on your heart. Would you talk to Him about what you've learned and what questions you still have? Will you get on your knees and pour out your heart—tell Him about your pain, your fears, and your joys?

# Notes

QUESTION 1

1. Luke Gilkerson, "Get the Latest Pornography Statistics," Covenant Eyes, last modified February 19, 2013, http://www.covenanteyes. com/2013/02/19/pornography-statistics/.

2. John Piper and Justin Taylor, *Sex and the Supremacy of Christ* (Wheaton, IL: Crossway, 2005), 26.

3. Roger Steer, *Hudson Taylor: Lessons in Discipleship* (Oxford: Monarch Books, 1995), 34.


QUESTION 4

1. Linda Dillow and Juli Slattery, *Passion Pursuit: What Kind of Love Are You Making?* (Chicago: Moody, 2013), 41.


QUESTION 5

1. Samantha Pugsley, "It Happened to Me: I Waited Until My Wedding Night to Lose My Virginity and Wish I Hadn't," *xoJane* (blog), August 1, 2014, http://www.xojane.com/sex/true-love-waits-pledge.


QUESTION 6

1. Portions of this chapter were adapted from Juli Slattery, *No More Headaches: Enjoying Sex and Intimacy in Marriage* (Carol Stream, IL: Tyndale, 2009).

2. Robert Byrne, source unknown.

3. Archibald Hart, *The Sexual Man* (W Publishing Group: Nashville, 1994), 79.

4. Ibid., 70.

## Question 8

1. Portions of this chapter were adapted from Linda Dillow and Juli Slattery, *Passion Pursuit: What Kind of Love Are You Making?* (Chicago: Moody, 2013).

2. Dr. Lewis Smedes, *Sex for Christians* (Grand Rapids: Eerdmans, 1994), 212.

3. This resource can be ordered at www.authenticintimacy.com.

## Question 9

1. Portions of this chapter were adapted from Linda Dillow and Juli Slattery, *Passion Pursuit: What Kind of Love Are You Making?* (Chicago: Moody, 2013).

2. Ibid., 101.

## Question 14

1. Scott Stanley, "Sliding vs. Deciding: Observations on Love, Sex and Commitment," *Psychology Today*, https://www.psychologytoday.com/blog/sliding-vs-deciding.

2. Glenn T. Stanton, "What's the Deal with Cohabitation? A Survey of This Decade's Leading Research," http://media.focusonthefamily.com/topicinfo/cohabitation.pdf.

3. Glenn T. Stanton, *The Ring Makes All the Difference* (Chicago: Moody, 2011).

4. Ibid., 106.

5. Scott M. Stanley, Sarah W. Whitton, and Howard J. Markman, "Maybe I Do: Interpersonal Commitment and Premarital or Nonmarital Cohabitation," *Journal of Family Issues* 25, no. 4 (2013): 496–519, doi: 10.1177/01992513X03257797.

## Question 15

1. ABC News, "Who's Likely to Cheat?" http://abcnews.go.com/2020/story?id=124040&page=1.

## Question 16

1. Portions of this chapter were adapted from Juli Slattery, *No More Headaches: Enjoying Sex and Intimacy in Marriage* (Carol Stream, IL: Tyndale, 2009) and Linda Dillow and Juli Slattery, *Passion Pursuit: What Kind of Love Are You Making?* (Chicago: Moody, 2013).

## Question 17

1. Portions of this chapter were adapted from Dannah Gresh and Juli Slattery, *Pulling Back the Shades: Erotica, Intimacy, and the Longings of a Woman's Heart* (Chicago: Moody, 2014).

2. Dolf Zillman and Jennings Bryant. "Pornography's Impact on Sexual Satisfaction," *Your Brain on Porn* (2006), doi: 10.1111/j15591816.1988.tb00027.x.

3. John Piper. *Desiring God: Meditations of a Christian Hedonist* (Colorado Springs: Multnomah Books, 2011).

4. C. S. Lewis, *The Weight of Glory* (New York: Harper One, 1976), 27.

5. Dirtygirlsministries.com.

## Question 19

1. Christopher Yuan, "Why 'God and the Gay Christian' Is Wrong about the Bible and Same-Sex Marriage," review of *God and the Gay Christian*, by Matthew Vines, *Christianity Today*, June 9, 2014, http://www.christianitytoday.com/ct/2014/june-web-only/why-matthew-vines-is-wrong-about-bible-same-sex-relationshi.html?order=&start=1.

2. Al Mohler, "God, the Gospel, and the Gay Challenge—A Response to Matthew Vines," http://www.albertmohler.com/2014/04/22/god-the-gospel-and-the-gay-challenge-a-response-to-matthew-vines/.

3. Oswald Chambers, *My Utmost for His Highest* (Grand Rapids: Oswald Chambers Publications, 1963),   .

## Question 20

1. Jill Savage, "Rebuilding Trust After an Affair," *Today's Christian Woman*, April 2015.

2. http://www.hopeandhealing.us/.

## Question 22

1. Jennifer Smith, *The Unveiled Wife: Embracing Intimacy with God and Your Husband* (Carol Stream, IL: Tyndale, 2015).

2. Freedomsteps.org.

## QUESTION 24

1. Couples Training Institute, "Myths and Truths of Marital Dysfunction," http://couplestraininginstitute.com/gottman-couples-and-marital-therapy/.

## QUESTION 25

1. Michele Cushatt, *Undone: A Story of Making Peace with an Unexpected Life* (Grand Rapids: Zondervan, 2015).

2. A. W. Tozer, "Tozer Devotional: Leaning Toward Heresy," The Alliance, last modified October 4, 2015, http://cmalliance.org/devotions/tozer?id=223.

3. Oswald Chambers, *Conforming to His Image* (Grand Rapids: Discovery House, 1950), 105.

4. Oswald Chambers, *Love a Holy Command* (Grand Rapids: Discovery House, 1989), 111.

5. Authenticintimacy.com.

# Acknowledgments

I am blessed to work with an incredible group of women at Authentic Intimacy. Linda Dillow and Hannah Nitz, you both give me input out of your love for the Lord and your "generational" lens. Joy Butts, you make up for my glaring difficulty with detail. Deana Williams, your creativity and sensitive heart bring to life the message God has given us. Thank you to Lauren Floyd for your help getting the manuscript ready to go.

Thank you to the team at Moody Publishers for supporting Authentic Intimacy in the endeavor to address such sensitive topics. Specifically, thank you, Judy Dunagan and Rene Hanebutt. You make working with Moody a joy! Thanks to Betsey Newenhuyse for your editorial help. Paul Santhouse and Greg Thornton, thank you for trusting us to honor God with these resources.

Michael, Andrew, and Christian Slattery, I'm sorry for the embarrassment it probably causes you to have a mom who writes about sexuality! You boys are the joy of my heart. I pray that God's love and truth sink deep into your hearts and are lived out in every area of your lives.